WHY MEN MUST LIE

PHILIP B. STORM

With a Foreword By
MOLLY BARROW, PH.D.

Barringer Publishing Naples, Florida April 2010
www.barringerpublishing.com
Cover, graphics, layout design by Lisa Camp
Editing by Elizabeth Heath

ISBN: 978-0-9825109-6-4

Library of Congress Cataloging-in-Publication Data
Why Men Must Lie / by Philip B. Storm

Printed in U.S.A.

DEDICATION

This book is dedicated to all women
who really need to understand men...
and are willing to accept the truth about them.
And to all men who already know,
even if they never admit it.

FOREWORD

The first knee-jerk reaction to Philip Storm's new book, *Why Men Must Lie*, divides along gender lines with women gasping audibly and with men managing suspicious little smirks. Philip Storm does not in any way endorse lying. He simply tells his stories and reflects on the choices many men have made. This book is essential reading for men and for the women who love them because lying often destroys relationships.

Depending on one's sex, I have the honor of introducing the reader to the important wisdom contained in the compilation of life stories called *Why Men Must Lie*.

To Females:

Calm down and listen to the man. He is revealing truths that initially seem breathtakingly heinous to the female nesting instinct and relationship goals. Often, a female selects a mate and then builds her entire world around that man, rendering herself inexorably dependant on his stability and his ability to have a healthy relationship or lack thereof. If a woman decides to add children to this scenario, her need for a strong, reliable relationship increases. A couple's desire to raise healthy, secure children may come at a cost of (historically) the woman's lifestyle, education, salary, retirement, adult friends, and occasionally, her sanity. Women have been known to stay home, give up a career, delay an education and assume most of the household duties as a means of attaining quality parenting time with her young children. She can only accomplish this level of stay-at-home-mom parenting if her spouse shares the same goals. If he says that he does, she will confidently jump out of a metaphorical airplane fully convinced that her partner will provide a parachute for the entire family. *Why Men Must Lie* cautions that, perhaps, Ladies, a reality check is required before you leap. According to author Philip Storm's chronicle, men think predominantly about sex, sex, and sex—not home, children and fidelity.

Why Men Must Lie can help you to understand why you may feel compelled to tell those fibs, even when it is not necessary. Since you were a child, you have been programmed to meet other's expectations and sometimes you fell short of those expectations and learned to lie. The pressure of taking full responsibility for a woman and a family, being "the man," is exhausting and riddled with resentment. Feelings of entitlement propel you down treacherous paths with severe relationship consequences. Your only solution may appear to be "just lie about it." This book will help ease the guilt of past lying and help you see the negative results of continuing to lie to people you truly love. *Why Men Must Lie* provides insightful relief and depth of understanding to the male dilemma and shares how other men who think about sex, sex and sex have handled their situations.

The reader will judge if quiet acceptance of lying is prudent or too difficult. Is it better to pretend that your partner will never lie to you and find yourself devastated when you discover the opposite is true? Or, is it prudent to approach love defensively, convinced that the sweet words of your lover are creative writing and protectively prepare to mistrust his every word and action?

If the brave work of Philip Storm exposes the subject of lying and helps to make open discussion possible, then relationships can become stronger as a result. Rather than wring your hands in guilt or flail your arms in angst, a couple can rework a relationship to reduce the requirement of man's absolute perfection and increase the independence of woman so that a lie between a man and a woman does not destroy their lives, finances and families.

More self-honesty and freedom to be fallible will reduce the need to lie to others. Can we allow a man to have weaknesses? Can we encourage our sons to learn and grow from their mistakes without shaming or bullying them into lying? Can we support women self-sufficiency from equal pay to free childcare and birth control?

Let love be about wanting each other's company rather than a desperate need to possess and control. Imagine if this concept spread to a national or global freedom from lying! Open your minds and your hearts to the truth about lying. *Why Men Must Lie* may set you free to be real.

Molly Barrow, Ph.D.
Clinical Psychology
Author of *Matchlines for Singles* and the *Malia & Teacup* series

CONTENTS

---

*"And, after all, what is a lie?
'Tis but the truth in masquerade."*

Lord Byron

INTRODUCTION

Why would an average man with no formal psychological training dare to write a book with such a provocative title, *Why Men Must Lie?* Why would a man even make such a statement, much less make it the subject of a book? Wouldn't the title alone cost him all his male friends and make all women afraid of him?

The answers to all those questions are quite simple. My life experiences have proven to me that the title is universally true and that it needs to be understood by women, period. All women can learn to deal more effectively with the men in their lives by understanding and accepting how true it is: men *must* lie to women!

Must is the key word in the title. I explore the ethical question of *should* with each story. Should a man attempt to communicate with a woman in a manner that reduces unnecessary conflict even if that means telling a lie? Or, should his brutal honesty wreck delicate bonds of trust and hurt the woman he cares for and desires? Men have fundamentally different feelings about virtually every aspect of life than women, but seldom are willing to confront these opposing feelings head on. Lying is a man's bridge between male and female reality.

I am truly a very average guy. I was in the army in the mid-1960s; I graduated from college and I went to work. After a reasonably successful international career I retired to Florida. I have been married more than once and I am now widowed. What then, qualifies me to write *Why Men Must Lie?*

Quite simply, I am one of those guys in whom other men confide. For more than fifty years, I have patiently listened to the men around me, and I have never breached a confidence.

Beginning in high school, then right through my military and college experiences and over a thirty-five-year business career, my male friends and associates poured their hearts out to me because they knew I kept my mouth shut. I've listened to men describe literally thousands of situations over five continents and one theme held true, *men lie to all the women in their lives, most of the time.*

I could not have predicted the need to write *Why Men Must Lie* when I began making notes to remember stories told by my male friends and associates beginning more than fifty years ago. A logical question is: Why would a young boy ever start making notes of such stories in the first place?

Before internet and television, people entertained each other by telling stories about everything imaginable. As a young boy, I often had the opportunity to listen to my extended family tell the stories of their lives to one another. With a total of twenty-four aunts and uncles, their spouses, and literally hundreds of cousins, the quantity and quality of the story telling sessions that took place at family gatherings was nothing short of amazing.

As the youngest of five children, I was expected to listen rather than speak during these family storytelling sessions. It was my father, however, who inspired me to begin making notes and reminders of the stories I heard.

"Somebody should write all of these family stories down so we don't forget them!" Dad would say. To please my father, I started writing notes and reminders of my family's stories almost as soon as I learned how to write.

As a *conditioned listener* and chronicler of events, it seemed natural that I continue making notes of memorable stories that boyhood friends told. This transcended into a life time of patiently listening to my male friends, making notes and reminders of their stories. Not just notes on stories about lying, of course, but notes on all kinds of stories. To maintain order, I began filing my story notes in the following major categories:

- Cars/Motorcycles
- Education
- Family
- Jobs/Careers
- Military Service
- Politics
- Religion
- Sports
- Wives and Girlfriends

Wives and Girlfriends emerged as the largest and most colorful of the categories, because when no women are present, men talk about the women in their lives more than anything else. The older men get, the more this is true.

As I collected and sorted these hundreds of *story reminders from Wives and Girlfriends,* the theory that resulted in *Why Men Must Lie* began to emerge. I've chosen only a representative selection of stories from the *Wives and Girlfriends* file to include in *Why Men Must Lie;* the remaining stories would have produced exactly the same conclusions.

For many women, their first reaction to the title may be, "That's preposterous! My husband would NEVER lie to me!" Or possibly, "Okay. Maybe most men, but not my guy! He's different!"

That attitude is precisely why it is imperative for men and women to continue reading.

As I listened to my male friends and associates, I observed that men told similar stories based on specific phases of their lives. These stories transcended race, religion, political conviction, education level, and economic standing. When I sorted and computerized these notes in preparation for writing this book, they fell into seven distinct age groupings.

These seven basic phases of men's lives are defined in fixed-year periods; the timing may in fact vary slightly, but the phases do not. Actions and reactions are differentiated by degree and intensity only; every man passes through each phase.

Why Men Must Lie focuses on an explanation of the seven phases of men's lives and how their interactions with women transition from boyhood to the elder years. Through a series of real-life stories, I make my case and explain why men's lying is so consistent, especially to the women closest to them.

The stories are true. Names and places have been changed to protect the guilty. If some sound oddly familiar it's because basic lying scenarios repeat themselves throughout people's lives and, sure enough, male creativity kicks in to explain things.

It begins with the male infant's earliest interactions with his mother that make him start fibbing to her almost as soon as he can talk. At an unimaginably young age, boys instinctively understand that their natural behavior does not please their mothers. They don't want to alter their behavior, but they are dependent on Mom for nearly everything. So they tell her what they think she wants to hear to get her to do what they want, beginning a pattern that lasts for life.

FIRST FLASH REACTION

This lying is rooted in a phenomenon that I identify as every male's *First Flash Reaction* to every woman he encounters throughout his life. This *First Flash Reaction* varies only in degree of intensity; it morphs predictably to fit specific situations. Men deal with it differently through the stages of their lives, but the patterns for all men are remarkably similar.

A reasonable response to the concept of man's *First Flash Reaction* may be to identify men you know who don't seem to fit the descriptions in the seven phases. Perhaps your father or your priest or rabbi, or even your brother seems the exception.

Man's *First Flash Reaction* to women assures that there are no exceptions. Some men are simply much better at lying than others, and better still at concealing their lying patterns, particularly from wives and girlfriends. All men believe they must become reasonably proficient liars to survive their interactions with the women in their lives.

The content of *Why Men Must Lie* is based totally on the male perspective. The concepts are not intended to be in any way provocative, but instead are candidly frank assertions of how men think and act…and lie to all the women in their lives.

I am in no way condoning or endorsing men lying to women. I am simply documenting what men do based on their own stories describing their behavior. Understanding what causes men to lie to women can be a most enlightening and therefore valuable introspection to successfully managing male/female relationships.

We'll begin by discussing the three basic types of lies that men tell women. Then we'll define the seven phases of men's lives and quantify lying frequency by lying type in each phase. An explanation of the four basic types of liars comes next.

Critical to understanding *Why Men Must Lie* is accepting and embracing the concept of every man's *First Flash Reaction* to women as defined in chapter five.

Next come chronologically organized true stories of how men begin and end their lives lying consistently to all the women they encounter. Please remember, whether the stories make you laugh, cry, or get mad, *they are true!*

Finally, I summarize my fifty years of listening to men's stories about their lying with conclusions that are eye-opening. With an improved understanding of the male experience, I believe you will concur with my conclusions.

THREE BASIC TYPES OF LIES MEN TELL WOMEN

All of the lies that men described telling women throughout their lives can be categorized into just three basic types. There is absolutely no limit to the creativity, justification, and rationalization men employ constructing each type of lie, but still, all fit into one of these fields:

- Overt Lies

- Borderline Lies

- Silent Lies

OVERT LIES

Overt Lies are the most easy to identify and understand. They are 100% untrue and usually are employed to position the man on exactly the opposite side of truth. A few examples help to define overt lying:

- A man enters his home from the garage reeking of cigarette smoke. His wife asks "Have you been smoking again?"

  He answers, "Absolutely NOT!" His wife knows he's lying, the man knows that his wife knows that he's lying, and still, he lies flat-out.

- A man returns home after midnight obviously inebriated, smelling of alcohol and laughing uncontrollably. "Have you been out drinking?" his wife asks.

"No. I had to stay late at the office to finish a project and one of the guys brought in a six-pack to get us through." He's lying, and both know it.

- A boy returns to a dance in the high school gym with lipstick on his cheek, sweating slightly. His steady girlfriend asks, "Where have YOU been?"

He answers, "I had to piss and the line was too long in the men's, so I went out back of the parking lot." Not even a good lie, stupidly overt.

It could be argued that Overt Lies are the least damaging because they are in no way believable. Still, men insist on absolutely lying overtly even when the truth may be simpler, and not necessarily all that damaging.

BORDERLINE LIES

A large percentage of the lies men tell fall into the Borderline category. These lies are much harder to discern because they often contain an element of truth. Borderline Lies tend to be more complicated and involved than Overt Lies. Men believe that they can always get away with *shading the truth* so Borderline Lies often are incredibly elaborate and involved. Examples are, understandably, more involved:

- A high school student arrives back home a little after 10 o'clock on a week night, past his curfew. Mom asks, "Johnny, you're late! Where have you been?"

Johnny answers, "Well, Mom, I've got that big science project, you know, and I went to the library with Steve's older brother so he could help us. He had the same assignment three years ago. Then some other guys were using the stuff we needed, and we didn't get to look at it until just before the library closed. I

15

should've finished my supper, like you told me, but, you know, I didn't, and I was hungry. So Steve and me and his brother stopped for a burger. Sorry I'm a little late."

Johnny did, in fact, go to the library, but it was with Suzie. No scientific research occurred. Then he walked Suzie home and they stopped for a burger. In Johnny's mind he hadn't lied. Not really.

■ A man returns from a three-day fishing trip with his buddies, exhausted, but clean-shaven and cheery. "How was the fishing? Catch anything?" his wife asks.

"No, nothing was biting! But we had a good time, you know, talking guy talk and drinking beer."

He had gone fishing with his buddies, but it started raining, so they went to a bar and met some local women. He hadn't done much *guy talking* and some things were biting! "I'm surprised you shaved way up there in the woods," his wife commented.

"Wanted to be fresh for you when I got home," hubby responds. Partly true, but mostly not; a classic borderline lying pattern.

■ A man comes home from his *employees only* office Christmas party slightly buzzed and smelling of fine cologne. "Well, you're home earlier than I thought you'd be," his wife comments. "Was the party fun? Do you have new after-shave?"

The man is prepared, "Got this Burberry Cologne from the gift exchange. My lucky day! Didn't want to stay too long. Those parties can get dangerous!" In fact he'd been at the party only an hour. His secretary had taken him to her place to give him his present, and the Burberry.

Borderline Lies and Overt Lies pale in comparison to Silent Lies in both frequency and magnitude of results.

SILENT LIES

Silent Lies are the ones women have the most difficulty dealing with and understanding. Silent Lies are all the feelings and opinions that men never express to their female partners, thereby creating the need to employ Borderline Lies and Overt Lies so often:

- A couple returns home from a night at the opera. The wife says, "Wasn't that wonderful? I've never enjoyed a performance more! Fix us a nightcap and let's talk about it!"

  "Okay, dear," hubby answers.

  In fact, he's dead tired and absolutely hated every minute at the opera house. "Let's buy season tickets for next year. Won't that just make our year?" his wife continues.

  He realizes how much his wife loves the opera, but for him it is true punishment. He remains silent, however, and his resentment builds; what can he do to get even?

- A man's girlfriend of five years comes home from work and announces, "Sweetie, you're going to be so pleased! I enrolled us both in a health club! It'll be my present to us! We can meet there after work or even get up early and go every morning. Isn't that great?"

  The boyfriend is furious, but he doesn't say so. "Was it expensive?" he asks.

  "Not really! And I know it'll help me lose these pounds I've put on!"

  "Okay." Accompanying his girlfriend to a gym was the last thing the man wanted to do, but he kept silent. Certainly, he wanted her to lose the weight and get back to the way she looked when they met, but he hated health clubs!

- For twenty years his wife had been dragging him to her parents' house for Thanksgiving. They always stayed three or four nights, and the two women went shopping on *Black Friday*, leaving him to deal with his extremely negative and grumpy father-in-law. "I booked our tickets for T-Day! Even better fares than last year. Won't it be fun?"

  Four days of absolute torture! "Yes, dear," he said.

As men mature, they find it progressively more difficult to tell women what they are truly thinking and feeling; what they really want. *Why Men Must Lie* explains how and why this phenomenon develops from the male perspective. It all starts far sooner in a boy's life than one might imagine.

Young boys start with relatively innocent Overt Lies and progress to Borderline Lies as they become more sophisticated. Silent Lies dominate in the later phases.

The 7 Phases of Men's Lives

Society often divides human life spans into three basic periods; adolescence, the teenage years and adulthood. To adequately explain *Why Men Must Lie*, however, it is necessary to further segment men's lives as follows:

Phase I	Ages 1-12	Innocence to Lying
Phase II	Ages 13-15	Lying Development
Phase III	Ages 16-21	Lying Perfection
Phase IV	Ages 22-35	Balancing Lying and Life
Phase V	Ages 36-55	Perfecting the Balancing of Lying and Life
Phase VI	Ages 56-70	Adjusting Lying to the New Realities
Phase VII	Ages 71+	Living with a Life of Lying

Phase I
Ages 1-12
Innocence to Lying

Men are not born liars. Lying develops as a necessary survival instinct as young boys interact with their mothers, trying to please them. As we'll see later, the lying usually starts with an absolutely innocent disclosure by a boy to his mother that causes her to overreact. The hardest thing for a male child to witness is his mom starting to cry. Covering up that innocent disclosure that caused the crying often results in the boy's first real lie.

Time and again I heard men recall their first departure from the truth as something that *just happened*. If the first small lie stops his mother's crying, that reinforcement of a *quick fix* no matter what he had to say, forms a pattern in the young man's brain. From a young age, males tend to seek quick, simple solutions. If a small fib stopped Mother's crying, that was a simple, perfect solution! If it worked once it'll probably work again; the pattern begins to develop. Men remember that later lies to their mothers often involved *covering up* confusing feelings about girls. This theme seems to continue through most men's lives.

The transition from lying to Mom to lying to teachers just comes automatically. The few men who recalled having male teachers in the lower grades remembered that lying to them was much harder.

Note: All pie charts and graphs are based on collected data of more than fifty years of unsolicited case studies.

PHASE I
AGES 1-12
LYING VS. TRUTH

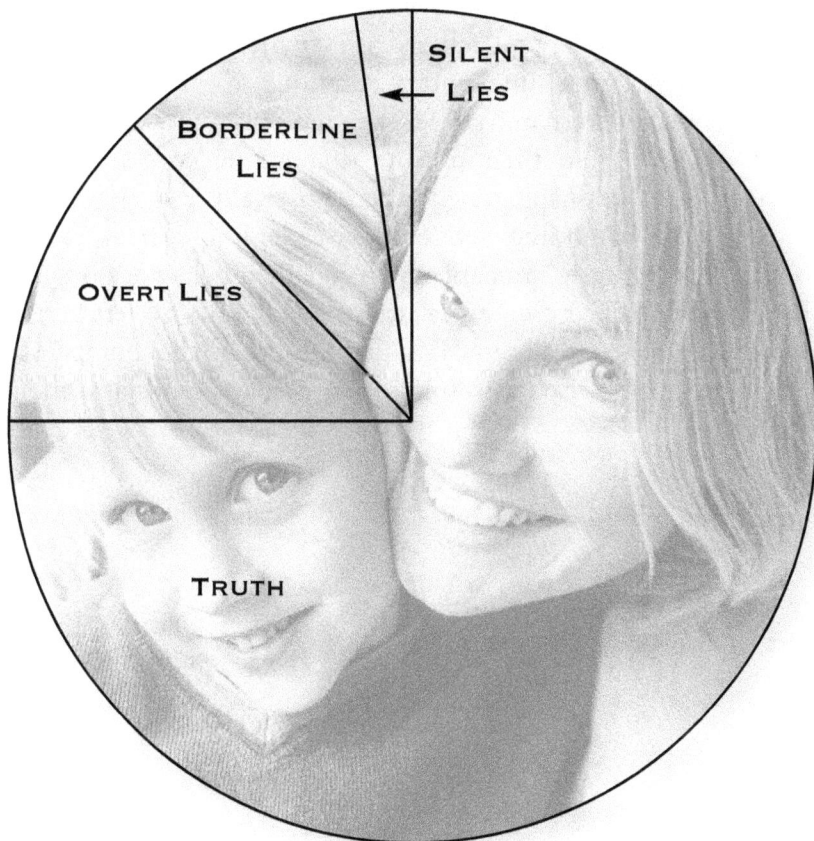

SILENT
LIES

BORDERLINE
LIES

OVERT LIES

TRUTH

IN THIS, THE FIRST PHASE, TRUTH IS TOLD **75%** OF THE TIME.

PHASE II
AGE 13-15
LYING DEVELOPMENT

Phase II can overlap a year or two in either direction depending on a boy's physical development. For most men, however, years thirteen, fourteen, and fifteen are remembered as extremely uncomfortable times when their mysterious, involuntary reactions to girls began. Of the hundreds of men who shared stories with me, only a tiny percentage had received *the talk* from their parents that might have helped them understand what was happening to them physically.

So, with little or no knowledge of the emerging sperm production capability that begins to dramatically change their behavior, boys in their early teens create their own explanations about almost everything. The opportunity, necessity really, for lying that this brings about prepares boys for their remaining years as results-oriented liars, especially about all things sexual.

PHASE II

AGE 13-15
LYING VS. TRUTH

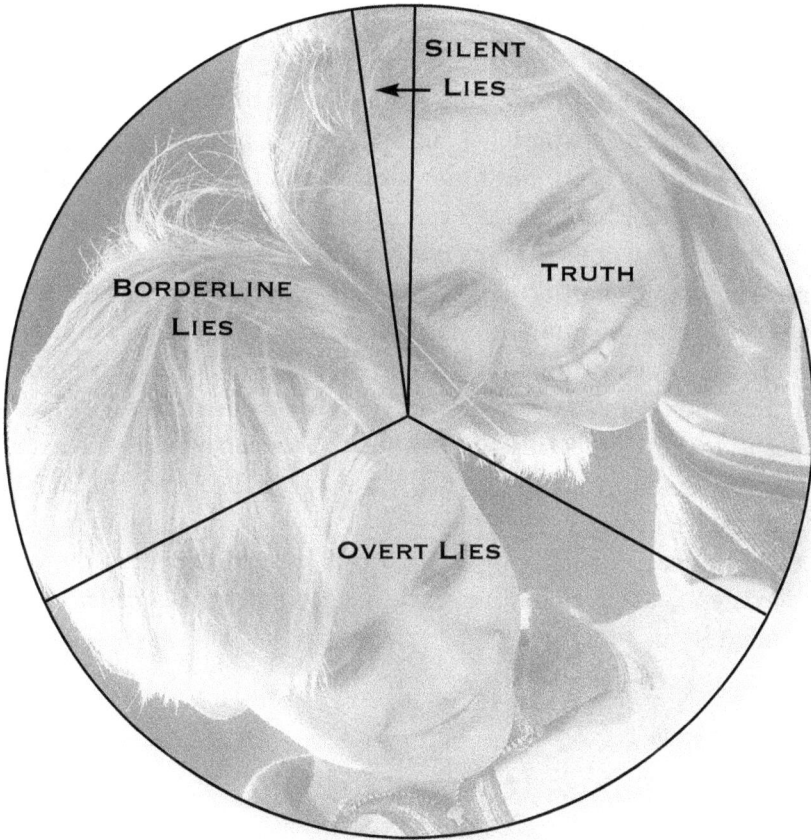

TRUTH TELLING SHRINKS DRAMATICALLY TO 33%,
WHILE BORDERLINE AND OVERT LIES BECOME MUCH
MORE COMMON, NEARLY EVEN WITH TRUTH.

PHASE III
AGES 16-21
LYING PERFECTION

By age sixteen every man who confided in me had graduated from the mystery and uncertainty about girls that began in Phase II to full-fledged, all-out, 24/7 devotion to *getting laid*. Achieving that all-important first sexual experience totally consumes the sixteen to twenty-one year old male. Based on his experience with lying to achieve quick, simple solutions that began with lies to his mother and teachers as described in Phase I above, the Phase III male quite naturally will tell any lie necessary to achieve his only objective, *to have sex*.

Once the young man actually does have sex, two completely diverse patterns of communication develop. The Phase III man brags constantly to all his male friends about his accomplishment, usually exaggerating the details and timing. Conversely, he will tell any lie necessary to all the females in his life, especially his mother, to *cover up* or *deny* the act. The lies the young man told that actually got the girl to say "yes" are filed away for future use.

This, of course, leads to lying about virtually every aspect of the young man's existence as he finds himself in nearly constant conflict with all the women in his life.

PHASE III
AGES 16-21
LYING VS. TRUTH

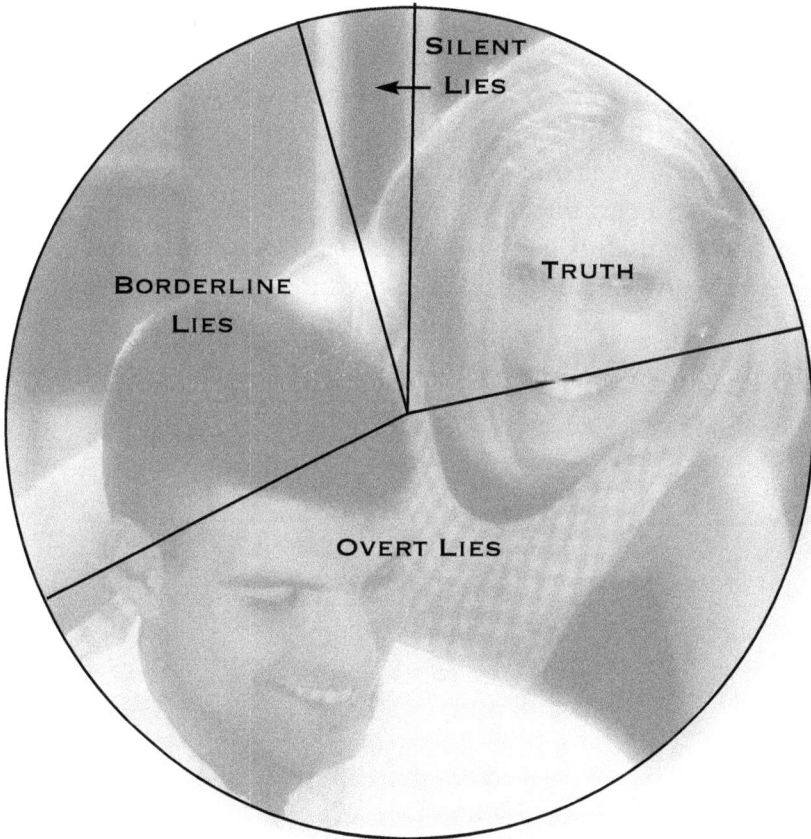

TRUTH TELLING SHRINKS EVEN MORE, NOW DOWN TO 23%,
AS OVERT LIES BECOME MUCH MORE PREVALENT.

Phase IV
Ages 22-35
Balancing Lying and Life

Men usually lose their virginity sometime during Phase III. A first sexual experience, however, only exacerbates a man's sexual desires. Following initial sexual contact, men in Phase IV become acutely aware of their *First Flash Reaction* to all the women with whom they come in contact. Lying either to achieve additional sexual conquests or simply to *cover up* or *conceal* their *First Flash Reactions* from wives and girlfriends gets elevated to an art form.

Men find themselves lying to women easily and conveniently about nearly everything, but always about everything concerning sex.

PHASE IV
AGES 22-35
LYING VS. TRUTH

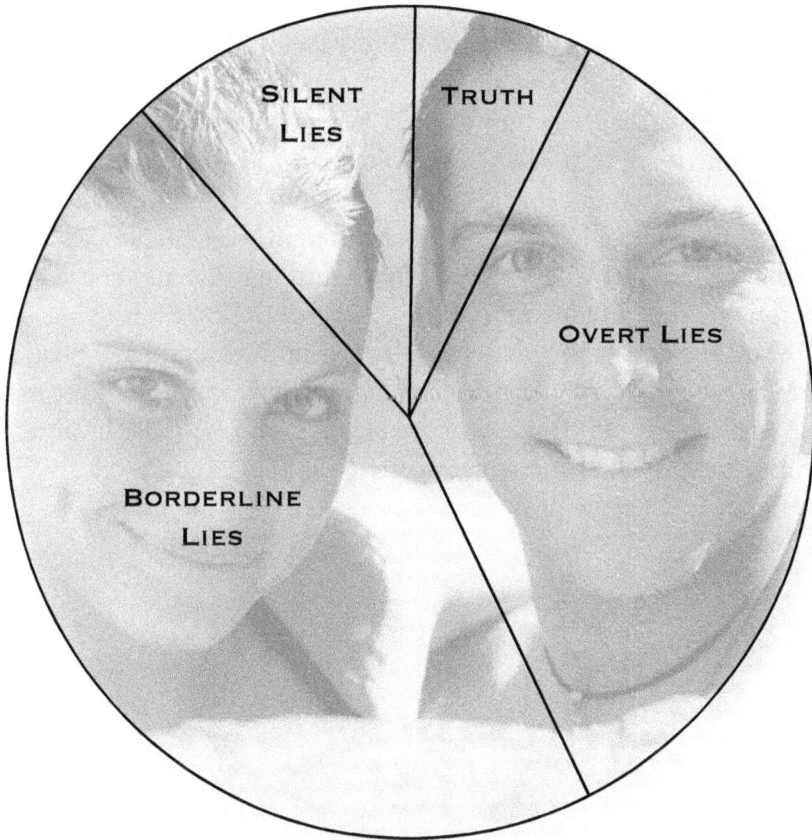

TRUTH TELLING BECOMES EVEN LESS COMMON,
AS BORDERLINE LIES INCREASE DRAMATICALLY.
SILENT LIES BECOME MORE FREQUENT.

PHASE V
AGES 36-55
PERFECTING THE BALANCING
OF LYING AND LIFE

Men recall telling lies in Phase V most vividly. By age thirty-six most men have had multiple female sex partners, but readily confess that "the more they have, the more they want." Life is relatively complicated for the average thirty-six to fifty-five year old man as he struggles to balance raising a family, building a career, enjoying his hobbies, and, most importantly, controlling his desire for different women. Not all men act on the latter, but every man who confided in me confessed to experiencing heightened *First Flash Reactions* during Phase V.

Toward the end of the phase, usually beginning around age fifty, many men describe the most intense *First Flash Reactions* of their lives as they long to experience different women *before it's too late*. The lies men tell during Phase V show amazing creativity as they employ years of lying experience in an attempt to *have it all*.

PHASE V
AGES 36-55
LYING VS. TRUTH

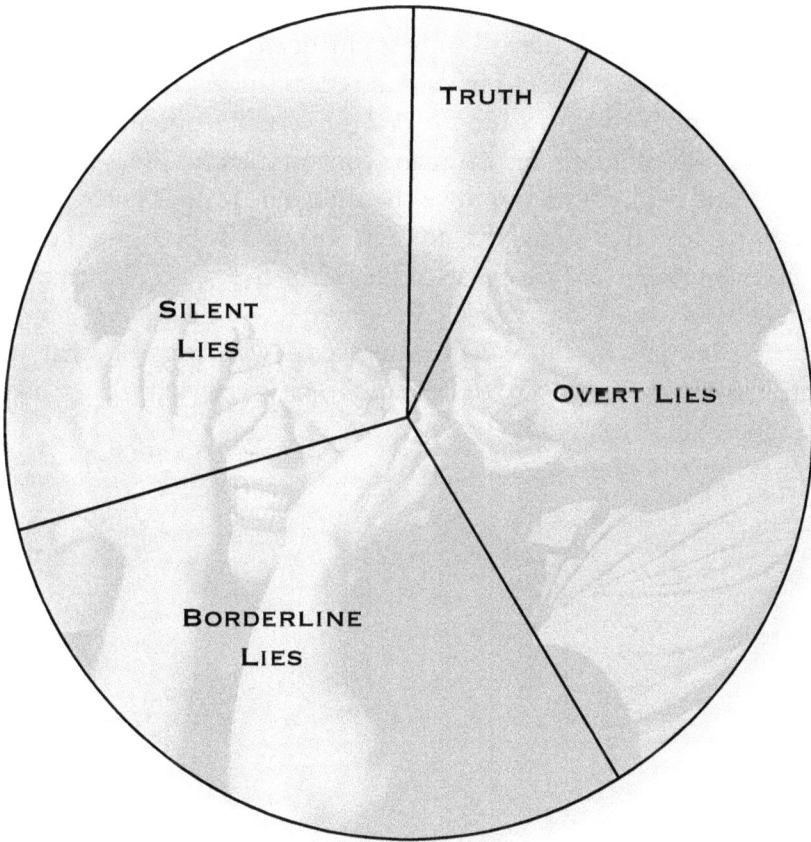

TRUTH TELLING REMAINS CONSTANT,
AS WE SEE A BIG INCREASE IN SILENT LIES.

PHASE VI
AGES 56-70
ADJUSTING LYING
TO THE NEW REALITIES

Stories from Phase VI reveal truly sophisticated lying techniques and tradecraft, set against backgrounds that reflect the *do it before it's too late* syndrome combined with a *what have I got to lose?* attitude. Lies told by 56-70 year olds often display the man's concern that his life is more than half over, and yet he's still not done the things he really wanted to do.

The much feared loss of ability to perform sexually becomes the man's reason to *do it before it's too late* with his thirty-five year old secretary or his neighbor's twenty-one year old daughter.

Stories from late in Phase VI are tempered with fears of what years of lying may mean to men as they face end-of-life issues, but the lying doesn't stop.

PHASE VI
AGES 56-70
LYING VS. TRUTH

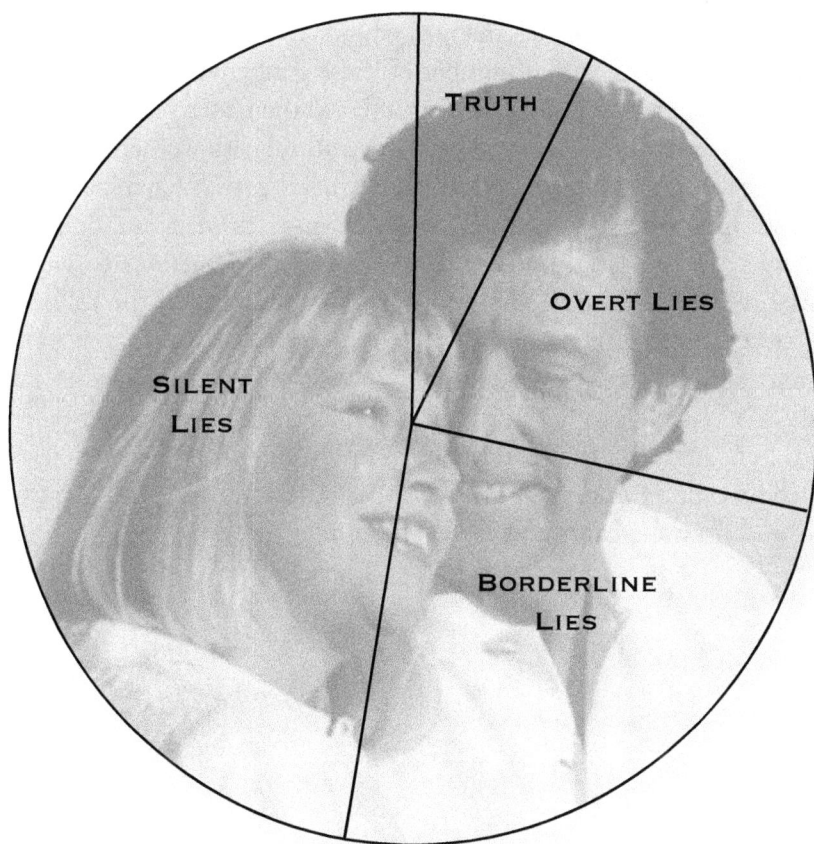

TRUTH

OVERT LIES

SILENT LIES

BORDERLINE LIES

SILENT LIES CONTINUE TO INCREASE
AS OVERT LIES BECOME LESS COMMON.

PHASE VII
AGES 71+
LIVING WITH A LIFE OF LYING

I have been fortunate enough to have maintained contact with lots of my old friends and past associates, many of whom are now in their seventies and eighties. *Circling back* with a number of these gentlemen has provided me with good insight as to how their lying affected their later years. Notice that Phase VII men actually become a bit more truthful with women as they age. This is because older men are so cranky they tell the truth for spite.

Questioning men in Phase VII always culminates with an inquiry as to whether the man is still affected by *First Flash Reactions* to women. Invariably, every Phase VII man told me some version of the following: "Hell yes! I'm old, I'm not dead!"

A particularly bright-eyed eighty-five year old man made this statement: "I've come clean with my priest and all my golf and poker buddies whom I cheated over the years. But fess up to the wife? Never! Hell, even now she wouldn't understand! Probably come after me with a butcher knife, and now she can move faster than me!"

PHASE VII
AGES 71+
LYING VS. TRUTH

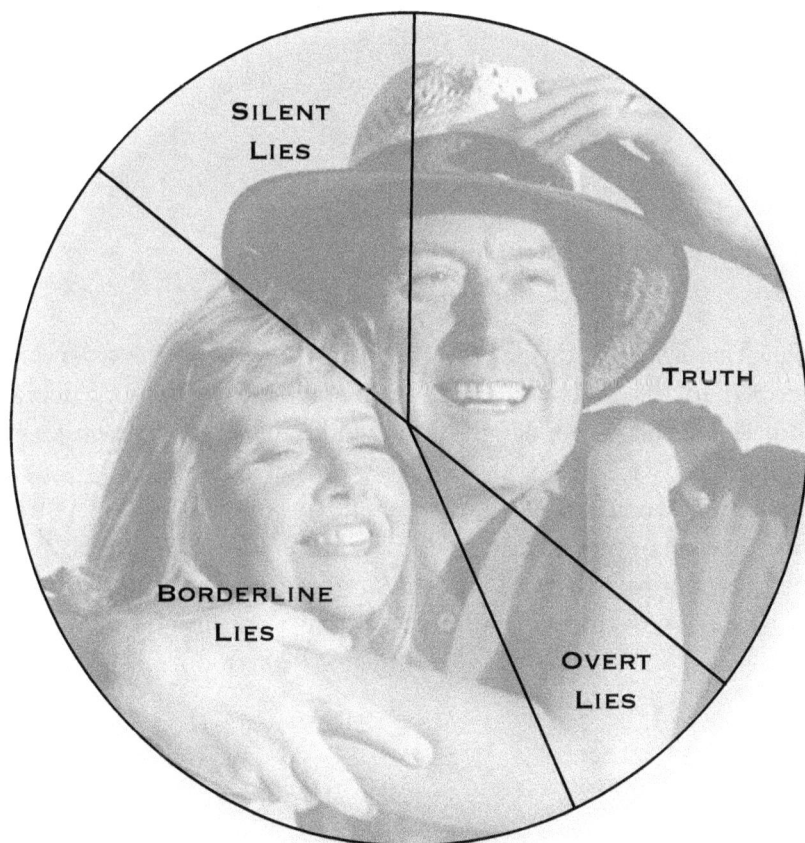

IN THIS, THE FINAL PHASE, TRUTH TELLING
MAKES A COMEBACK, SILENT LIES ARE LESS COMMON
AND BORDERLINE LIES BECOME MORE POPULAR.

WHY MEN MUST LIE
TO WOMEN
PROBABILITY CHART

Why Men Must Lie divides the following stories into the seven phases described in the previous pages. Following is a probability depiction summarizing the percentage of time men lie to women in each phase of their lives.

Describing when and how often men lie to women is relatively straight forward. Explaining exactly *why* they lie requires considerably more effort. The stories in *Why Men Must Lie* give excellent insight as to why; the last section of the book summarizes why they *must* lie.

WHY MEN MUST LIE TO WOMEN

PROBABILITY CHART

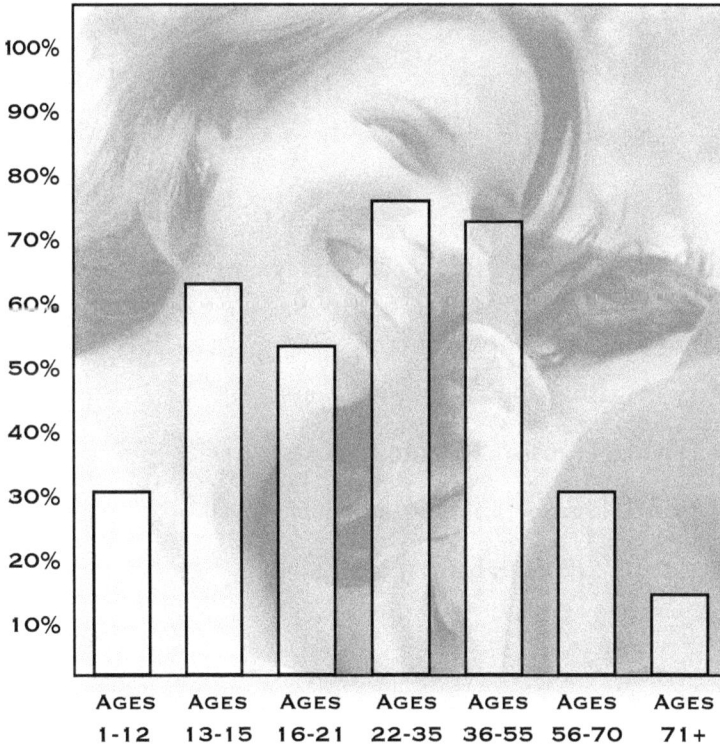

	100%
	90%
	80%
	70%
	60%
	50%
	40%
	30%
	20%
	10%

AGES 1-12   AGES 13-15   AGES 16-21   AGES 22-35   AGES 36-55   AGES 56-70   AGES 71+

PERCENTAGE OF THE TIME MEN LIE TO WOMEN, PER AGE/PHASE GROUP.

THE 4 BASIC LIAR TYPES

There are almost as many variations of how and when men lie to women as there are men. Studying and analyzing the hundreds of stories of men lying from my *Wives and Girlfriends* file suggests, however, that men fall into four basic types of liars:

- Type I: Bold and Aggressive Liars

- Type II: Consistent, Careful Liars

- Type III: Reluctant, Sporadic Liars

- Type IV: Fearful, Infrequent Liars

A WOMAN'S POTENTIAL TO INFLUENCE THEIR MAN'S ABILITY TO BECOME TRUTHFUL BASED ON THE TYPE OF LIAR

The following pie chart divides men into the four basic types of liars based on my fifty years of data. Depending on the type of liar, a woman has a higher or lower likelihood of influencing his behavior.

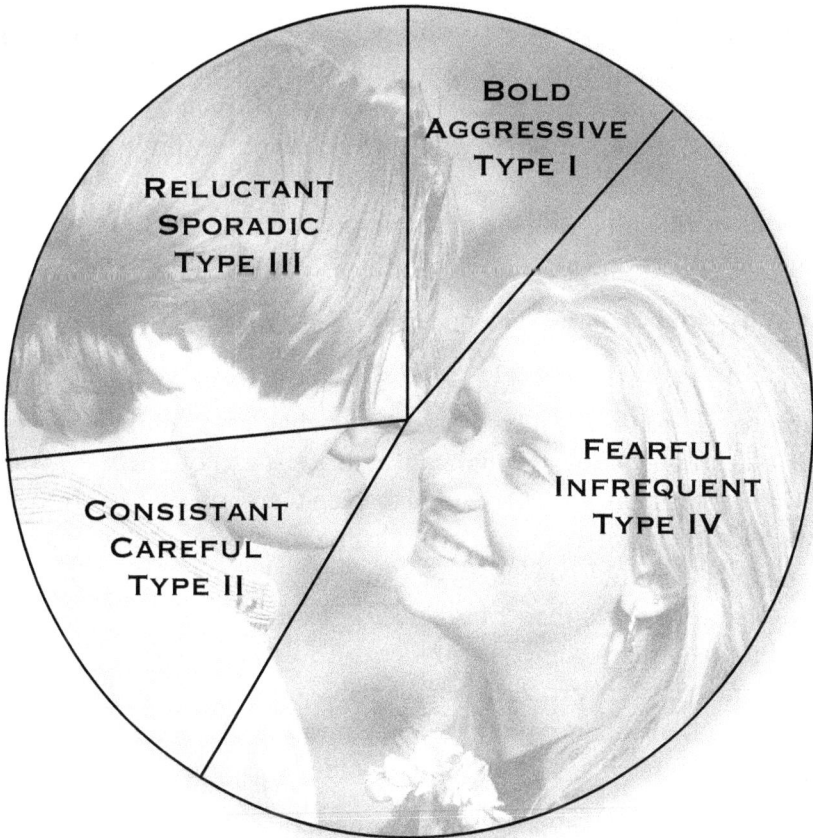

BOLD AGGRESSIVE TYPE I

RELUCTANT SPORADIC TYPE III

FEARFUL INFREQUENT TYPE IV

CONSISTANT CAREFUL TYPE II

TYPE I: BOLD AND AGGRESSIVE LIARS

Bold and Aggressive Liars are self-confident, successful men who simply cannot resist their *First Flash Reactions* to woman. The more affluent this type of liar becomes, the more women he is likely to pursue. These men have egos bigger than Texas, and usually make themselves the center of attention wherever they go. They drive Ferraris and BMWs, and talk the loudest at cocktail parties. High-profile athletes, politicians and CEOs often fit into this liar type. Interestingly, there is a subset within Bold and Aggressive Liars consisting of low-profile, under-the-radar men who nonetheless acquire many female sex partners throughout their lifetimes by lying through their teeth about virtually everything. Bold and Aggressive Liars develop early and never change, often blossoming in their mid-'50s and *acting out* right through the remainder of their lives. These are the guys who, usually to no one's surprise other than their previous wives, wind up marrying thirty year old trophy wives in their sixties and seventies. If a woman is married to a Bold and Aggressive Liar, her odds of changing him are nearly non-existent.

TYPE II: CONSISTENT, CAREFUL LIARS

A notch down from Bold and Aggressive Liars, Consistent, Careful Liars are self-confident men usually somewhat less materially successful who still must follow through on at least some of their *First Flash Reactions* to women. They are careful to keep their indiscretions from their wives and other girlfriends for fear of losing their comfortable home base. Consistent, Careful Liars like to play the game cautiously by maintaining a much lower profile than Bold and Aggressive Liars. They possess big egos, but keep them somewhat under control. Consistent, Careful Liars stay married until they're sure their womanizing won't destroy their careers or threaten their financial well-being. Consistent, Careful Liars are only slightly less difficult to live with than Bold and Aggressive Liars.

TYPE III: RELUCTANT, SPORADIC LIARS

Reluctant, Sporadic Liars are everyday Joe's who long for the occasional affair, but seldom follow through. Given the right, supposedly *safe* opportunity, these men will definitely give in to their *First Flash Reactions,* but lack the self-confidence to push as hard as liar Types I and II. Still, Reluctant, Sporadic Liars average one to four extramarital sexual liaisons throughout their lives. They openly talk to other men about how they wish they had the courage to do what they really want to do, i.e. have more affairs like their heroes in Types I and II.

TYPE IV: FEARFUL, INFREQUENT LIARS

Fearful, Infrequent Liars are the guys other men refer to as *hen-pecked.* Their desires to follow through on *First Flash Reactions* are inhibited by fears of consequences. They readily admit, however, to lusting after other women almost as much as men from the three more aggressive liar types. They live with the effects of being constant silent liars because they just don't possess the courage to do what they really want to do. Fearful, Infrequent Liars tend to live vicariously through the escapades of men in Types I and II. They say "yes dear" much of the time, but seldom mean it.

All men naturally fit into one of these four types of liar categories for their entire lives, unless a woman can somehow alter this basic male characteristic. Women will have little difficulty in deciding which liar type their man fits into, but admitting which type he is, even to herself, is far more difficult. The graph on page 40 is a depiction of the probability of being able to coerce honesty from men by liar type as determined by my *circling back* to hundreds of his confidants.

Clearly, women's potential to influence their man's ability to become truthful varies dramatically based on the type of liar he is. If the man is a Bold and Aggressive or Consistent, Careful Liar, there is only an 8 or 13% probability, respectively, that anything a woman can say or do will bring about a transition to honesty. These men are hard core, *First Flash Reaction* implementers who are extremely unlikely to feel the need to change their ways, period.

Reluctant, Sporadic Liars have only a 27% probability of becoming truthful. Fearful, Infrequent Liars are the most likely to stop lying under effective coercion at 43%. Certainly better odds than Types I and II, but extremely challenging nonetheless.

A WOMAN'S PROBABILITY OF BEING ABLE TO COERCE HONESTY FROM MEN BY LIAR TYPE.

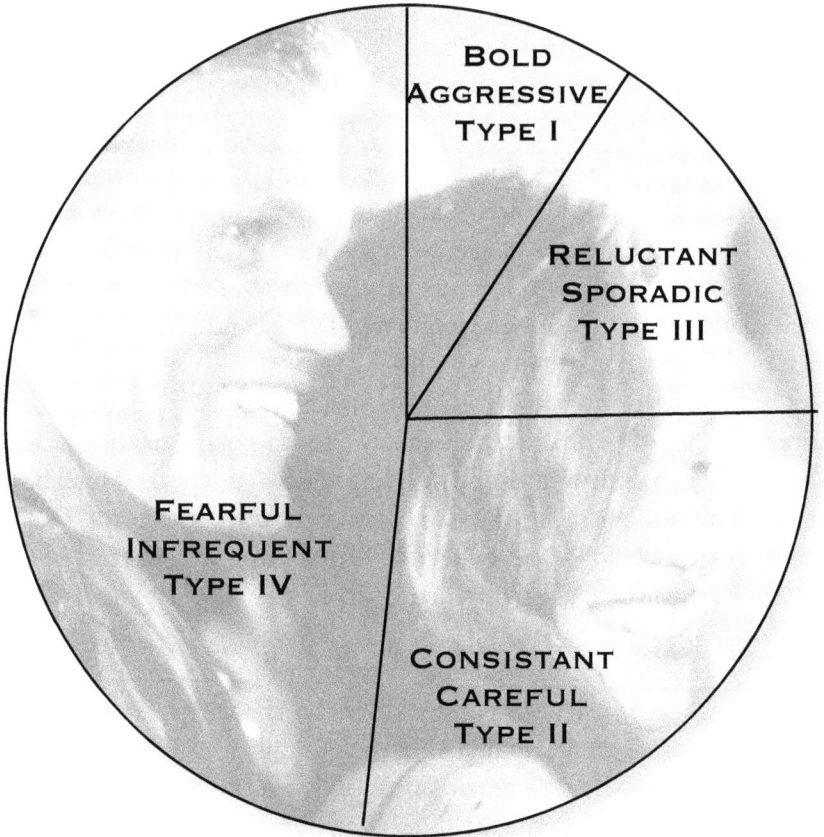

BOLD AGGRESSIVE TYPE I

RELUCTANT SPORADIC TYPE III

FEARFUL INFREQUENT TYPE IV

CONSISTANT CAREFUL TYPE II

THE FIRST FLASH REACTION THAT MAKES MEN LIE

Every man who confided in me readily acknowledged that he'd experienced *First Flash Reactions* to women for as long as he could remember. Although there were differences in how each man described his own personal *First Flash Reactions*, sufficient commonality emerged to construct the following definitions by phase.

In the most basic terms the *First Flash Reaction* is a male's involuntary, natural first brain impulse in the presence of a female.

PHASE I: *FIRST FLASH REACTION*, AGES 1-12

From birth, baby boys immediately identify their mother as the source of their needs fulfillment. Beginning with basic nourishment right through first life lessons, boys see their mothers coming toward them and learn to expect certain behaviors that are very different from those of their father figures.

Flash: There's Mom; she's gonna feed me and hold me.

A little later on:

Flash: There's Mom; she gonna bathe me, dress me up, and take me out for a walk to show me off to her friends.

Later still in the phase:
Flash: There's Mom; she's gonna yell at me for playing in the mud!
Still later, maybe age nine:
Flash: There's my principal, Mrs. Brown. She's gonna paddle me for pulling Linda's hair! And my teacher, Mrs. Tinker, sent me to Mrs. Brown's office!
The boy sees a female and automatically anticipates behavior from her that is very different from that of the men he observes. He begins to comprehend that he needs to alter his own natural behavior to please females, or lie about what he's really thinking and feeling.

PHASE II: *FIRST FLASH REACTIONS*, AGES 13-15

Puberty is kicking in; hormones are starting to work. Differences in behaviors between females and males that he learned to expect from birth are influenced by forces within him that he doesn't understand.
Flash: There's cute little Amber who I used to throw spit balls at. Why is she smiling at me? Why do I have a strange feeling between my legs?
Later in Phase II:
Flash: Holy Christ! Look at Amber now! She's got boobs! Why am I sweating? Oh, God, it's getting hard again! I gotta sit down!
But at home:
Flash: Please, God, don't let mom see that I get a hard on every time her friend, Mrs. Haze, walks in the room!

PHASE III: *FIRST FLASH REACTIONS*, AGES 16-21

Physically the boy has become a man. His body is in full-blown sperm production mode, causing him to think constantly about sexual release.
Flash: Ms. Kean has the greatest legs in the world! And she smells fantastic! It's not right for a teacher to be so gorgeous!
Later:
Flash: God, you can take my life tomorrow, just let me have Jeannie tonight! If I don't get laid I might as well die!
Then, after he finally loses his virginity:

Flash: There's Judy! What a body! Would it be different with her than it was with Jeannie? Man, I gotta find out! And there's Annie! I bet she's better than either of them!

Immediately following his *First Flash Reaction* the Phase III male ponders:

Flash: Why aren't these girls as horny as I am? What have I got to do to get them interested? What can I do? Or say?

PHASE IV: *FIRST FLASH REACTIONS*, AGES 22-35

By now the young man has had a sufficient number of sexual partners to know that he wants more. It doesn't matter if the woman is his boss, his best friend's wife, or the woman in the cubicle next to him at work. If she's female and even a little bit attractive, he fantasizes about what she would be like in bed!

Flash: My boss Lorraine has the greatest tits in the world. Love to see 'em in the flesh just once. Oh Christ! She's just given me more work!

Later in Phase IV:

Flash: There's Nina, my wife's best friend. Most perfect ass I've ever seen. Man, what would it be like to caress that beautiful backside just once? Okay, more that once!

Still later in the phase:

Flash: My mom's friend Sue must be sixty, but what a body. Wonder if the older gals know how to do it different?

PHASE V: *FIRST FLASH REACTIONS*, AGES 36-55

By Phase V, men's lives are complicated and confused. Despite their myriad of responsibilities and obligations, Phase V men have *First Flash Reactions* that are essentially the same as in Phases II through IV.

Flash: Wow! Would you look at Katie Johnson's figure! What I wouldn't give for just one night with her. Don't care if she is my boss's boss. I'd give that a shot any time.

Occasionally, the *First Flash Reaction* is negative, but no less a male's involuntary, natural first brain impulse.

Flash: Judge Flanders is so fat I'd hate to have to see her naked. But she does have a pretty face. Wonder if she's gonna rule in our favor in this case?

PHASE VI: *FIRST FLASH REACTIONS,* AGES 56-70

The mature men of Phase VI still experience *First Flash Reactions,* but are beginning to be affected by concern for their comfort as they get older.

Flash: Man, she's hot! Better cool it though. She can't be worth having to split my retirement income with the misses!

PHASE VII: *FIRST FLASH REACTIONS,* AGES 70+

Seniors are actually beginning to be slightly more truthful with women some of the time as the concept of consequences combines with low sperm production.

Flash: Boy, if I were ten years younger I'd be on her like a bear on honey! Wonder if she minds bald guys? But if she told Margie I'd propositioned her, my wife would kill me!

Of course, men don't always act on their *First Flash Reactions.* Most of the time that first impulse passes quickly to a more acceptable, conditioned behavior that society expects. But the *First Flash Reaction* is still what every man initially feels every time he encounters a female. From birth he has been conditioned to the fact that his mother, then his female teachers, then the girls he so wanted to have sex with, don't think like him.

Telling the truth or candidly expressing his wants and desires invariably was modified by every female he had to deal with, beginning with his mother. To get the desired reaction from women, he's learned to tell them what they want to hear, truth be damned.

"It is not difficult to deceive the first time, for the deceived possesses no antibodies; unvaccinated by suspicion, she overlooks lateness, accepts absurd excuses, permits the flimsiest patching to repair great rents in the quotidian."

John Updike

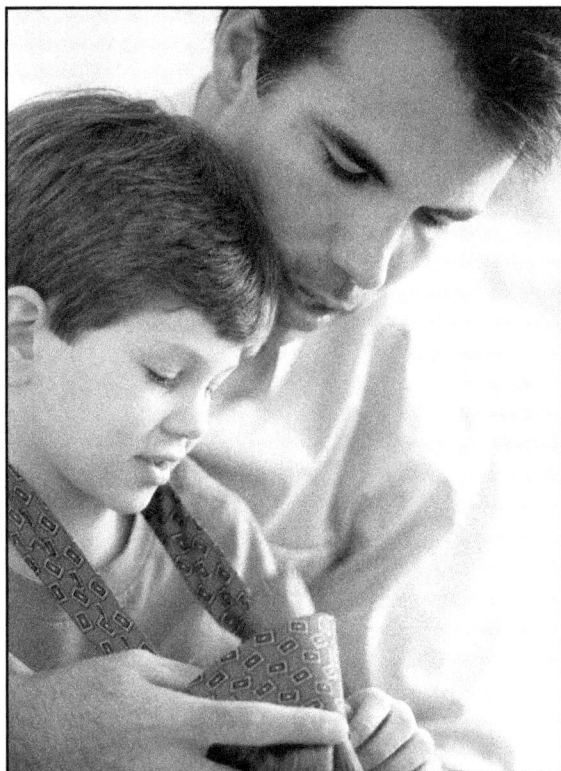

PHASE I
AGES 1-12
INNOCENCE TO LYING

JUNIOR'S FIRST LIES TO MOM, *NOT DAD*

Baby boys are born dependent on their mothers or some other female for care and affection. Of course, babies' fathers or other significant males may contribute to their early needs fulfillment, but it's their mother on whom young boys learn to depend.

During the early years, little boys' lives are centered on their interactions with what their mothers choose for them. They are fed and dressed, kissed and pampered, and generally catered to by a woman who loves them. Very early on, little boys learn that the caregiver also has expectations of them. She expects smiles and hugs in return, and she wants them to wash their hands even when the hands don't appear to need cleaning.

Expectations quickly escalate to speaking softly and being polite. Mothers want their sons to be sensitive and gentle, sweet and kind.

Minding what their mothers ask of them brings toys and ice cream and often, a puppy.

A typical four year-old boy sees his mom as the absolute center of his universe. If he makes her happy, all good things come to him. Conversely, if Mom gets angry she often calls on Dad to discipline him, maybe even spank him!

So, for many men, the first memory of fibbing involves answering a question from his mother in such a way as to avoid something unpleasant.

"Did you just pee on the side of the house?" screams his mother on the morning of his fifth birthday. "We have guests coming for your party!"

First dilemma. The evidence is clear. There's a steamy yellow liquid running down by the drainpipe which he playfully jumps back from just as Mom asks her question.

Flash: "But Mom! I couldn't get the back door open and I couldn't make it if I went through the house! I didn't want to go on your rug!"

There they are, the first lies. Insignificant, really. They were actually sort of true.

"Where did you learn to do that? Your father doesn't pee outside! I'm so ashamed! What if the neighbors saw you? I'm just going to have to take back all your birthday presents!"

Junior observes that his Mom is truly upset with him. So he tries to explain.

Flash: "Mom, Jimmy and his dad do it all the time! Right out behind the garage when we're playing catch! It's too far to get to the bathroom from there!" The lies continue.

"I don't care what those people do! You can't ever go to Jimmy's house again! Wait until your father gets home! Go up to your room right now! And stay there!" His mom is still yelling at the top of her lungs and she's actually starting to cry!

Flash: "Mom, I'm sorry! I'll never do it again! I promise!" More lies roll off Junior's tongue as easily as breathing as he offers to alter his natural behavior to regain his mother's favor.

"Go to your room and wait for your father to get home!"

The five year old trudges up the stairs to his room, trying to comprehend what just happened. His heretofore perfect mother screamed at him for peeing! Just because he was outside! Clearly, Mom didn't buy the story about the stuck back door. Or the distance from the bathroom. And she didn't care that other guys do it, even Jimmy's dad. But the worst thing that happened was that Mom started crying.

Junior's world had begun to change. His natural behavior no longer pleased his mother. Just as he was about to start crying too, his mom comes to the door.

"Can I come in, honey?"

Now Junior is totally confused. Five minutes ago Mom was screaming at him and sent him to his room to wait for Dad's spanking. Now here she is asking if she can come in to see him in that sweet voice he knows so well.

"Sure Mom."

"Honey, you really couldn't get in the back door? And you didn't want to go on the carpet?" Mom asks.

Flash: "Uh, yeah," Junior replies. Lies number nine and ten? Keeping count becomes difficult.

His mom comes over to where he's sitting on his bed, kisses him and says, "It's okay, baby. You couldn't help it. I won't tell Dad, but just never do it again, promise?"

Flash: "Sure Mom." Lie number eleven.

Later that day when his dad gets home from work junior is waiting. "Hey Dad! Hi! I had a great birthday party with lots of kids! And presents! But Mom got real mad at me!"

"Why's that? What'd you do?" Dad asks.

"You know how we always pee behind the garage when we're playing catch? I peed on the side of the house and Mom got real mad. She was gonna have you spank me when you got home, but then she changed her mind."

"She saw you pee on the side of the house?" Dad asks.

"Yeah."

"Don't pee outside when she's looking. Women don't like things like that," his father advises and opens his evening newspaper.

"Are we still going to the ball game tomorrow, Dad?" Junior asks.

"Sure. Why wouldn't we?" Dad answers.

So on his fifth birthday junior told his mom several fibs, lies, and Dad took him to the Cincinnati Reds game the next day. Reds beat the Cubs six to one.

Three years later, junior got a really cool catcher's mitt for his birthday from Dad. As they were playing catch out behind the garage his dad said, "Hey, I gotta pee. Watch around the corner and make sure no one's looking."

"Coast's clear, Dad! Watch for me! I gotta pee, too."

As father and son resumed their game of catch Junior asks, "Dad, remember when mom got so mad at me on my fifth birthday when she saw me peeing on the house?"

"Uh, yeah, I think I remember that. Wanted me to spank you, right?"

"Yeah, but she forgot about it by the time you got home. Dad, I told Mom a couple of fibs that day. I told her Jimmy Smith and his dad peed outside. Not you and me. Then she made me promise not to do it again. But we do it all the time. Is that wrong?"

The father realizes that he is about to have the first really serious talk with his son. "Hey, let's take a break. Grab us a couple of Cokes from the fridge in the garage. Let's sit on the wall and talk."

As Junior fetches the cokes, father considers his predicament. "Son, we need to have a really serious talk," Dad begins.

"You mean about the birds and the bees, Dad?"

Stunned, his father asks, "WHAT? What do you know about that? What have you heard?"

"Well, not anything, really, but Jimmy Smith says our dad's are gonna explain things about girls to us real soon. Is that what we're gonna talk about?"

"Uh, not quite yet, son. I want to talk about the lies, er, fibs you told Mom when you peed on the house. There are some things women just don't understand about us guys. They just see things different and get upset about all kinds of things we do naturally. But you should never fib to Mom or me. When you do something Mom doesn't like, just say you're sorry. It'll be alright."

"Should I go tell her I'm sorry again, Dad?"

"Uh, no. You told her then and it probably wouldn't be a good idea to bring it up again. Finish your Coke, let's play!"

"Dad, when are we gonna talk about girls?"

"Later, son. You're not old enough yet. Now show me that fast ball!"

"WHAT DID YOU SAY?" LIES

Way earlier than their mothers are willing to acknowledge, little boys become enamored with adult language. Usually around the age of 6, but sometimes as early as three or four, young males hear older boys and men say words that their mom's refer to as *bad*.

There is something absolutely magical that occurs when a boy's mother forbids the use of *bad words*. A deeply hidden gene within all Phase I males immediately identifies those bad *words* as the most fascinating sounds in all the English language. The stronger Mom reacts to a forbidden word, the more absolutely irresistible that word becomes. He files those forbidden, *bad words* away in his brain, innately understanding that they can be employed to gain immediate attention in almost any situation.

As Junior begins storing up words like *shit, damn* and *hell* they make him feel somehow older and more grown up. After all, it's the older males that he so looks up to who use these words. The boy, of course, wants to be just like those older guys, the sooner the better.

"Hey, Mom! Good morning. What the hell are we having for breakfast?" 7 year old Johnny asks.

"WHAT? WHERE DID YOU HEAR THAT WORD? You are never to use the word "HELL" in this house, young man! Where did you hear it?" Mom demands.

Flash: Wow! That got her attention! "Uh, maybe Dad?" A lie; it was his pal Billy's older brother yesterday at the park.

"YOUR FATHER does not use that kind of language! And neither will you! I don't EVER want to hear you use "hell" again. Do you understand? Do you hear me?"

Flash: "Okay, Mom. Sure. I didn't know it was bad," Johnny says. Two more lies. Of course he suspected it was a forbidden word and now he knows for sure. And he has no intention of not using it again.

"What's for breakfast, Mommy?" Johnny softens his approach.

"Well, I was going to fix your favorite pancakes before you used that REALLY BAD word. I guess you can still have them if you PROMISE not to use bad language."

Flash: "Okay." Man, I wonder what Mom would have done if I'd used some of those other cool words Billy's brother uses.

A few months later Johnny was back at the park with his buddy Billy, trying to get into a basketball game that some older guys (ten) had organized. They were standing between two courts watching some teenagers play while they waited. One of the better teenage ball handlers got off a nifty pass to a teammate cutting to the basket, but the potential shooter took his eye off the ball and the pass sailed by him out of bounds.

"FUCK, man! If you can't catch my FUCKIN' passes get out of the game!" the ball handler yelled.

"FUCK you, man! I scored twenty-two points! How many you got?" came the reply. The opposing team inbounded the ball and play continued, but Johnny and Billy were staring wide eyed at the two players who had used the F word. Neither boy said anything.

A few minutes later a couple of the ten-year-olds had to leave and Johnny and Billy were reluctantly allowed in the game as replacements. On opposite teams, of course.

"Awright, kid, can you at least guard your buddy so he doesn't get an easy lay-up?" the lead player on Johnny's team asked.

"FUCK yes," Johnny answered.

And so little Johnny, age seven, added the F word to his emerging list of forbidden sounds. It got him into big trouble the very next day.

The weather had turned cold and Billy was over at Johnny's house playing with the slot cars his dad had set up in their basement. Johnny got to practice all the time, so he easily won every race as Billy struggled to master the art of braking for the curves so as not to run his slot car off the board. The boys were quite engrossed in their races and didn't notice that Johnny's mom and grandmother had finished folding the laundry and were standing by the stairs, watching the boys play.

After Billy ran his favorite slot racer off the track for about the twentieth time Johnny said, "FUCK man! If you can't keep the fuckin' car on the track, you oughta quit racing!"

Johnny's grandmother passed out. His mom had to catch her mother to keep Grams from hitting her head.

Flash: "Oh, shit! I didn't see you there, Mom!" Johnny cried.

"BILLY! GO GET YOUR MOTHER! I NEED SOME HELP RIGHT NOW! Johnny, I swear to Christ I'm going to blister your bottom!" His mother screamed. Johnny ran up the steps right behind Billy and followed him all the way home out of pure fear.

"MOM! JOHNNY'S MOM NEEDS you over there right away!" Billy said.

"WHY? What happened?"

"Johnny's grandma passed out! Right in the basement!"

As Billy's mom ran to help Johnny's mother, she called out to Billy's sixteen-year-old sister, "Janie, call 911 to Johnny's house! Grams passed out!"

"Where you going?" Billy asked Johnny.

"To hide, damn it!" Johnny said.

Billy followed his mother back to Johnny's house, but Johnny ran across the street and hid under Mr. Houser's porch. Way in the back where no one could see him. It was from this location that Johnny watched the ambulance arrive at his house.

Shit! Damn! Hell! I'm in trouble now! Johnny began to make up stories to explain his use of the F word, but he knew he was in big trouble when they found him.

By 7:00 pm, the whole neighborhood was out searching for Johnny. Though his grandmother did not leave in the ambulance and was, in fact, helping to look for him, Johnny remained hidden under the porch. Just as it was getting dark, and he was getting really hungry, a police officer shined his flashlight up under Mr. Houser's porch. "Okay, kid, come on out."

Uh-oh! And Dad's right there in the driveway. "Please let me stay here, officer," Johnny begged. "I'm gonna catch a beating when Dad sees me! Please!"

But Johnny's dad had seen the officer talking to him. "Get out from under there, NOW! In the house young man. Officer, thank you so much. We'll be fine now."

"You gonna paddle him, sir?" the officer asked.

"Probably."

"I would," the cop said.

But first came something Johnny dreaded more even than a spanking from his father. He had to face his mother and grandmother. His father marched him into the front room where his mother was silently sobbing, until she saw her son.

"Did you tell your father what started this awful afternoon for our family?" his mother asked.

Flash: "Uh, not yet Mom. I'M SORRY!"

"STOP IT WITH THE PHONY 'I'M SORRY!' Jim, your son used the F WORD! TWICE! It made Mom faint!"

Flash: "No, Mom! I said foo NOT the F word! Really! I would never use bad words! I know I'm not supposed to!" Johnny pleaded.

"YOU USED IT TWICE! AND NOW YOU'RE LYING ABOUT IT! Jim, DO SOMETHING!"

Johnny got a spanking. Of course, he had no idea what the F word meant, but he understood completely the affect it had on his mother, and grandmother. "Dad, ALL THE GUYS say the F word. Why can't I?"

"Because it upsets your mother. And Grams! Son, I don't want you using that kind of language either. You're gonna hear older boys use all kinds of bad words, but that doesn't mean it's okay. You saw the affect on Mom; just don't use them around women!"

"Dad, what's it mean?" Johnny asked.

"Son, it refers to something you're not old enough to know about, yet. So just drop it," his father said.

"You mean like sex, Dad?"

"ENOUGH! We'll talk about those things when you're older!"

Johnny knew it was time to shut-up, but he'd made the associations: *Sex was about bad words and women couldn't stand to hear about it!*

BIRTHDAY PARTY FIBS

Many men remember pre-teenage birthday parties as some of the most uncomfortable, embarrassing moments from their youth. Marty Bassman, a sixty-one year old retired physician from Philadelphia, recalled one of his worst early memories.

Marty woke on the morning of his eighth birthday with feelings of excitement and apprehension. His mother had organized a birthday party featuring pony rides for Marty's little friends, complete with cowboy hat favors and a western barbeque. A combination of children from his neighborhood, as well as the private grammar school Marty attended, would be arriving around noon for a day filled with games, hot dogs, ice cream and birthday cake, plus pony rides. So why the apprehension?

Just a few days previously, Marty's mother decided to expand the list of invitees from twenty to thirty-two. The additional twelve birthday party guests were all girls from Marty's class. Even worse, Marty's arch-enemy, Mary Ann Brown, who everyday at school made fun of Marty's larger than average ears, had agreed to attend. Now his mother had decided that Marty must stand at their front door and welcome every single guest, thank them for coming, and present them with a cowboy hat! Black hats for the guys and white hats for the girls was Marty's mom's idea.

"Mom, I HATE ALL THOSE GIRLS! Why did you have to invite them, anyway? It would've been so much fun if just my buddies were coming!"

"Now, Marty! We've been through all this before! You're eight years old now! It's time you learned to properly socialize with all your classmates, especially the girls!" his mother told him. "Besides, you've been invited to two birthday parties for girls in your class, so it's only proper they be invited to your party!"

"Aw, Mom! What girls' parties? I didn't know I had to go to girls' parties too!"

"The first one is Mary Ann Brown's party next Saturday! Won't that be fun?"

"MOM! I HATE HER! She's like the worst kid in my whole class! She teases me all the time! I'm not going to her damn party!"

"WATCH your mouth, young man! You ARE going to her party, I've already said "yes." Now get moving! Your father and I want to give you a special present, so come on downstairs. Wash your face and brush your teeth first!"

Oh, man! What if Jimmy and Robert find out I gotta go to Mary Ann's party next week? I'll hear about THAT forever!

Marty's party dread was temporarily forgotten when he got downstairs. His parents got him the new bike he'd hoped for, plus a really cool cowboy pistol and holster set. "GEE! Thanks! These are great! Can I take it for a ride, right now? With my guns on?"

Out on the sidewalk, Marty's pleasure ended immediately. "Hey, Marty!

I hear that brat Mary Ann Brown is coming to your party! Why'd you invite her?" Robert asked.

"I didn't! My mom did! I hate her!"

"Yeah yeah. If you hate her, she wouldn't be coming to your party! I think she's your girlfriend!" Robert said. "Maybe you should just have all girls at your party!"

"I'm gonna punch you! Mary Ann is NOT my girlfriend!"

That afternoon as his little friends arrived, Marty stood at the front door and handed out hats under his mother's close supervision. Every time he tried to leave his post to go to the backyard where his buddies were playing, his mom took hold of his shoulders and held him by the door. Then came his most dreaded moment.

Through the screen door Marty saw Mary Ann Brown and Kathy Rice exit Kathy's mom's car and start up the steps. At that exact moment his buddy Robert came running across the yard and bounded up the steps right behind Kathy and Mary Ann.

Aw Christ! Why now, Robert? "Hi Kathy. Hi…er…Mary Ann."

As his mother greeted Kathy and Mary Ann, Robert was making faces at the girls behind their backs.

"'Lo, Robert. Welcome." Marty had to welcome every guest per his mother's instructions. Then it happened. Mary Ann Brown, his arch-enemy and class nemesis, turned back to Marty right in front of Robert, and kissed him on the cheek!

"Happy birthday, Marty," Mary Ann said. She and Kathy then ran on out to the backyard where the other kids were lining up for pony rides.

Both Marty and Robert stood in shock at Mary Ann's kiss. Then Robert recovered and started laughing.

"Wasn't that sweet?" Marty's mom said, over Robert's howling.

Marty Bassman was too shocked to respond. Robert headed for the backyard, undoubtedly to relate the story of Mary Ann's kiss to all Marty's guests.

"Well, son, it appears Mary Ann is fonder of you than you are of her!" Marty's mother said. "Was that the first kiss you ever got from a little girl?"

Flash: "YES, MOM!" In fact, it was not, but Marty wasn't about to disclose that to his mother.

When their last guest, Billy, arrived, Marty and his mom walked back to the party with him. Of course, Robert had told every kid at the party about *the kiss.*

"Marty and Mary are sweethearts! Marty and Mary are sweethearts!" came the chant from the little girls at the party. Most of the boys just pointed at Marty and laughed.

But Marty's eighth birthday problems were just beginning. Later that afternoon while the kids were seated having cake and ice cream, Mary Ann positioned herself next to Marty's mother. Marty saw her whispering in his mother ear, and then he saw his mother turn absolutely white. Marty's mother excused herself from the party, leaving a couple of the other kids' mothers to keep watch over the celebration.

Oh God! What did Mary Ann say to mom? I think I'm in big trouble! Why, oh why did Mom have to invite girls to my party?

Marty's mother was absent from the party for some time. When she rejoined the party she was even paler than when she left.

By 4:00 pm all of Marty's party guests had gone home, except for Mary Ann Brown. When Marty went inside, there was Mary Ann and her mother seated next to both Marty's parents. Still pale, Marty's mother said, "Son, Mary Ann tells me you and she have been playing *doctor.* Is that true?"

Uh-oh! Oh, shit! She TOLD! "Marty, your mother asked you a very important question. Answer it, RIGHT NOW!" his father said.

"Uh, yeah, I guess," Marty said.

"But Mrs. Bassman! All we do is take our clothes off and hug," Mary Ann said. Mary Ann Brown's mother passed out right there on the couch.

When Mrs. Brown came to, she and Marty's mother interrogated both children. After careful questioning, the parents determined that Marty and Mary Ann hadn't done anything *awful,* but Mrs. Brown and his mom were still terribly upset. It was agreed that one of the two children would *resign* from their grammar school class to keep them separated.

When Mary Ann and her mother finally left, Marty's parents really bored in on him. "You said you HATED Mary Ann! You told me at the front door not three hours ago that was the first time you'd been kissed! Now we find out you've been playing doctor for over a year! How could you have done this? Why did you lie to me about *hating* Mary Ann? Oh,

Marty, I'm so ashamed of your behavior!" his mother said. Marty's dad just stared at him.

Flash: "But mom! It was all her idea!" Marty said.

Fifty-three years later Dr. Bassman still squirmed as he told his story.

"So, Doc, was it really all Mary Ann's idea?"

"Of course not. But I couldn't tell my mother the truth, could I?"

FIRST GIRLFRIEND LIE

Many American men recall early instances of lying to their mothers about Valentine's Day issues, usually between ages ten and twelve. There's a great deal of pain, embarrassment, and confusion associated with that first Valentine dilemma.

Years before adult situations cause men to lie to women concerning their true sexual desires, boys find it impossible to be honest with their mothers and teachers about their emerging physical attractions to girls.

Bobby sat in math class wondering if he'd get that bicycle he so wanted for his eleventh birthday. He'd had the misfortune to be born on February 13th, and his family usually gave him presents that were for birthday and Valentines. *Why couldn't I have been born in March or April? Then I'd probably get separate presents. Only worse time for a birthday would be just before Christmas.*

"Bobby Mace! I'm TALKING to you! Are you paying attention? I asked you to give your answer to question number nine. Now tell the class your solution." Miss Elbert said.

"Uh, what?" Bobby asked.

The whole class erupted in laughter. Bobby felt his face turning red, but he really had no idea what Miss Elbert was talking about. He'd been day dreaming about bikes ever since the class started.

"Bobby Mace! Did you do your homework? We're on question number nine, volume of the rectangle, and I want your solution."

Flash: "I-I-I'm still thinking about question eight," Bobby said. A lie, of course.

"Really! Did you not understand Beverly's solution? How can we help you?" Miss Elbert asked.

Her question brought more laughter from his classmates and Bobby was truly embarrassed. "I didn't really hear her answer, Miss Elbert."

"Beverly, please repeat your solution. Maybe Mr. Mace will listen this time." More laughter.

Beverly, Miss Elbert's pet, methodically explained her solution one more time.

"Got that, Bobby? Now it's your turn. Solution to number nine, if you please, Mr. Mace."

"Uh, I guess I didn't get that one done, yet," Bobby tried.

"Mr. Mace! Stand in the corner facing your classmates, and focus on every word for the rest of this class or go to the principal's office. Your choice."

Bobby went to the corner to the delight of his hissing classmates. When Miss Elbert had her back to the class, most of the students made faces at him. When math class finally ended, Miss Elbert stood directly in front of Bobby and said, "You had better come prepared tomorrow, mister. I know your mother personally, and I'll call her if you don't start participating in this class."

Just when Bobby figured the morning couldn't get any worse, Beverly White, math genius and teacher's pet, walked up beside him. "Bobby, you're one of the smartest kids in class! Why don't you do better? Anyway, I wanted to give you this."

Beverly handed Bobby a pink envelope that actually had a pink ribbon holding it shut. "Happy Valentines Day and Happy Birthday!" Beverly said.

Bobby stopped dead in his tracks and stood staring at the envelope as Beverly walked away.

"What's that?" Larry Hart asked from just behind Bobby.

"NOTHING!"

"Yeah, it is! Looks like a Valentine's Day card to me! Or maybe it's the answer to question nine!" Larry said.

Bobby turned and punched Larry right in the face, dropping his card in the process. He then lunged at Larry and both boys tumbled back into Miss Elbert's classroom.

"BOBBY MACE! STOP THAT RIGHT NOW! You're in big

trouble, mister! MR. BROWN! Come help me with these two," Elbert shouted.

Mr. Brown, the boys' gym teacher, separated Bobby and Larry and marched them right to the principal's office. Larry had a trickle of blood running down his chin from a split lip.

"Mr. Mace and Mr. Hart! You two here again! Now what?" Principal Jones asked.

"Seems they were fighting over this," Mr. Brown said, handing Bobby's Valentine to Jones.

Flash: "It's not mine!" Bobby blurted out.

"Is too! I saw Beverly White give it to him! When I asked about it, he punched me!" Larry said.

"Is that what happened, Mr. Mace?"

"Uh, sort of," Bobby said.

"The envelope does have your name on it, Mr. Mace. You started all this? Let's hear your version," Principal Jones demanded.

"He was teasing me about that!" Bobby said, pointing at the Valentine.

"And that gave you cause to hit Mr. Hart? So you did swing first? That right?"

"Yes, ma'am."

"Mr. Hart, go clean up and get back to class. Mr. Mace, sit down. When did you receive your Valentine? Did you give Beverly a card?" the principal asked.

"HELL… Er, I mean *no* ma'am! I did not! She just surprised me after math class and put that in my hand! I didn't do anything!"

"Actually, you did. You started a fight over a Valentine. There's just no excuse for that kind of behavior. I'll expect you to give your parents a full and accurate explanation of what happened this morning, and I'll be in your math class tomorrow to listen to your apology to Mr. Hart and the entire class. I'm calling your mother right now to alert her about your misbehavior. Understood, Mr. Mace?"

"Yes, ma'am."

That afternoon Bobby struggled with how to explain the situation to his mom. He knew he'd have to tell his dad later when he got home from work, but Mom would be waiting at the door.

"HOW COULD YOU BEHAVE LIKE THAT? What in the world got into you? Talk, mister," Bobby's mom said.

Flash: "Larry was teasing me, Mom! He just wouldn't stop! I had to shut him up!"

"What was he teasing you about?"

Flash: "Just stuff, Mom! About my answers in math class." No mention of Beverly's Valentine card; in fact, no mention of Beverly at all.

"Is that all, Bobby?" his mother asked.

Flash: "Yeah, Mom, Larry just kept making fun of me!"

"Mrs. Jones mentioned that there was a card involved, Bobby. A Valentine card from Beverly White! Is that true?"

Oh, shit! I can't believe that bitch Jones told mom about that! How could she?

Flash: "Mom, I've never even talked to her and she gave me that damn card, right in front of Larry! The whole school knows about it by now!" Bobby's lies to his mom rolled easily off his tongue.

"YOU WATCH your language, young man! Don't you ever say "damn" in this house again! Wait until your father gets home! Go to your room, RIGHT NOW!"

It's all Beverly's fault! How'd I know she'd get me a damn card? Do I have to get her one now? Damn! "But Mom…"

"GO!"

Bobby and Beverly had been flirting with each other for over a year. They even held hands occasionally if no one was looking. Lately, Bobby had been getting an erection when they held hands. There was no way Bobby was going to tell his mom any of that! She just wouldn't understand.

Two hours later, Bobby's father knocked on his door. "OPEN UP! NOW!"

"Uh, hi, Dad! Sorry I'm in trouble again."

His father slammed the door shut and then softly asked, "Did you win?"

"Yeah, Dad! I caught him a good one! Right in the kisser. Just like you taught me!"

"What'd you tell your mom?"

"I told her Larry was teasing me. He was, but Mrs. Jones had already told Mom I got a Valentine card from Beverly White," Bobby said.

"What'd the card say?" his dad asked.

"Aw, Dad! You know! Junk about being friends and stuff."

"Is Beverly your girlfriend?"

"Uh, sort of. We talk sometimes. She always wants to hold hands!" Bobby said.

"And you didn't want to tell your mother about Beverly? Have you kissed Beverly yet?" his dad asked.

"COME ON, Dad!"

"That's not an answer. Yes or no. Have you kissed her?"

"Yeah. A couple of times," Bobby confessed. "But Dad! You can't tell Mom!"

ADMIT NOTHING

For most males, the relatively sweet and simple life of boyhood changes dramatically somewhere between their ninth and twelfth birthdays. Seemingly overnight the penis, that heretofore was only a soft obsession, begins to become hard and erect without any warning at all hours of the day and night. Usually the young man's parents have put off having *the talk* with him. The first mysterious emission from his penis scares the boy silly.

If he hasn't received direction and instruction about his sexual maturing from his parents or through the limited reproduction information offered at school, the young man is bewildered by that first release. Should he tell his parents? Can he ask his buddies if it's happened to them? Is it normal? What does it mean? Is he a man now?

His whole life suddenly is consumed with questions that he fears to ask. When will it happen again? How can he control it? And why does his penis get hard every time he sees a pretty girl? Can she see that he has an erection?

But the worst worry of all is, "How can I hide this from Mom?"

The answers to all those awful questions come, over time, in a variety of ways and from an assortment of sources as the young man struggles to understand all the changes occurring to his body. The physical changes, of course, set off a more dramatic shift in how the young man's brain begins to work.

All he can think about is that *thing* that happens to his penis, especially when he sees a pretty girl.

As the nightly emissions become more frequent, the young man knows his mother is bound to see the soiled bedding sooner or later. Something near panic invades his mind as he dreads that awful moment when Mom discovers that something is happening to him.

One morning at breakfast, in front of his father and sister, his mom casually says, "Honey, when you have an accident at night, just put your sheets in the laundry basket. Are you okay?"

Accident? Just like that it's out in the open! He nearly chokes on his oatmeal. He simply cannot respond.

But good old Dad picks up on what his mother said and announces, "Maybe we should have that talk, ya know?" His father actually winks at him!

"What are you guys talking about?" asks his younger sister.

"Nothing, dear. Your brother is just growing up, that's all," Mom replies.

If the incident described above seems preposterous, think back. If you had a brother, particularly an older brother, a variation of this discussion probably happened in your home, too. The point is, from the time that a male reaches physical maturity as defined by his body's ability to produce and emit semen, his ability to be honest with women completely disappears.

Why? Because from that moment on, at first sub-consciously, and then absolutely overtly, the young man's *First Flash Reaction* to every woman that he encounters for the rest of his life, other than his mother and sisters, will be to qualify them as a potential sexual conquest.

If this sounds absurd, if you want to slam shut this book and put the concept of the *First Flash Reaction* out of your head immediately, you are female. Men know how absolutely true it is, but they never talk about it to the women in their lives.

Let's continue to explore the seven phases of men's lives to further examine this *First Flash Reaction* concept.

PHASE II
AGES 13-15
LYING DEVELOPMENT

LYING COVERS LIES

Although much has been written about how early young people begin having sex, the fact is the majority of young men don't experience normal intercourse on a regular basis before their mid to late teens, or later. Men who are forty and older today often did not experience intercourse until their late teens or early twenties.

Phase II, ages thirteen through fifteen, is the time of hardest adjustment to their burgeoning sexuality for most males. Once sperm production begins, the urge to find a sexual outlet becomes the driving force in every young man's life. Many males discover masturbation early in Phase II. They then spend an inordinate amount of time shamefully giving themselves pleasure, all the while doing everything in their power not to be discovered.

What men remember most about this phase of their lives is how all-encompassing was the drive for sexual release. Secondarily, they remember the lengths they would go to hide their aroused condition and nighttime emissions from their families, especially their mothers.

During their lying development years, maturing males struggle constantly with how to deal with the women around them. Female classmates, pretty young teachers, even their friends' mothers begin to arouse that uncomfortable longing for physical contact. Boys aren't even sure what it is they want from women, but they know they want something.

All of this mounting frustration is exacerbated by their friends' creative descriptions of their own sexual experiences. Never mind that on some level, boys sense that the braggarts are, in fact, telling tall tales. Just the thought that other young men might possibly be doing what they so desperately want to do themselves drives boys to distraction.

Despite the unrequited, constant longing for their first sexual experience, most young men are afraid to initiate any advances toward the women around them. Teasing questions from friends and family are particularly hard to deal with.

"Billy, were you talking to that pretty little Callahan girl when I picked you up from school today?" his mother asks.

Flash: "NO!" Billy blurts out, afraid that somehow his mother had been able to read his mind when she saw him talking to Sally.

"Really? I could've sworn you two were head-to-head," Mom continues. "She sure has a cute figure."

Now Billy is truly terrified. Could his mom possibly know he was staring down the front of Sally's sweater? That he was asking Sally about a math problem, but was fantasizing about giving one of those beautiful breasts just one little feel? Did his mom notice his erection as he slid into the back seat? Worse, did Sally notice?

Flash: "No she doesn't. I mean, I never really noticed. She's just in a couple of my classes. She's really good at math." The lies just ooze right out of Billy.

"So you were talking to her! Is she your age?"

"Yeah, I think so," Billy says. Her birthday is October 10th.

"Bill, has your father talked with you yet about, you know, boys and girls? I mean about becoming a man? Or what that means?"

Flash: "Uh, no. But that's okay! We learned that in science class at school," *Billy tells his mom. A total fabrication.*

"Well, that's good. Just ask us if you have any questions, okay?"

Flash: "Sure, Mom. What's for dinner?" Billy wants only to change the subject away from an uncomfortable conversation about sex, even though he has a million questions he wishes he could ask.

That evening at the dinner table Billy's mom says, "I think our son has a girlfriend! He was talking to that cute little Sally Callahan when I picked him up from school today!"

"He talks to her all the time," Billy's little sister confirms. "I saw them holding hands!"

Flash: "YOU DID NOT! She's not my girlfriend! Leave me alone!" Billy yells.

And so continues Billy's string of lies to his mom. Of course Billy was holding Sally's hand. That's not all he has been holding.

Billy's father tells himself that he's got have *that talk* with his son real soon.

STUART LIES HIS WAY TO CAMP

Stuart Blumenfeld knew his mother was on to him. Hard as he tried to hide his masturbation from his family, Stuart was sure the escalating frequency with which he pleasured himself was becoming obvious. He stood looking in the mirror, examining the acne on his face, completely frustrated with everything about his life.

Why am I still so short? And so damn chubby! Why does my skin look red and greasy? Why can't I stop masturbating? Why do all the other guys have girlfriends? Shit, shit, shit!

"Dear, are you about done in the bathroom? Other people need to use it too, you know! Don't be late for school, Stuey!" Stuart's mother, Dr. Judith Ross-Blumenfeld, said.

As Stuart exited the bath his mother was right there, waiting for him. "Are you okay, Stuey? Can I do anything for you? Did you use the acne scrub I got you? Is your homework all done?"

Jesus H. Christ! She's gonna drive me crazy!

Flash: "Yes Mother, I'm fine."

"How did the SAT tutoring session go? Do you want more math help? Should I get Becky Stienworth back to tutor chemistry?" Dr. Ross-Blumenfeld was determined that Stuart would follow the family tradition and become a medical doctor. "Did you enroll in those summer classes like we discussed?"

Flash: "SAT prep is going fine, mom. I've never gotten anything but A's in math. I guess I could use help with chemistry," Stuart said. Actually, he got A's in chemistry, too, but Becky Stienworth's body was something Stuart fantasized about constantly. Just three years older than him, Becky was a truly gifted student, about to complete her first year of college at 17. Not really a pretty girl, Becky did have world class breasts and a tiny waist complimented by a backside that Stuart considered perfect. In the summer, Becky tanned to a gorgeous golden-brown.

"Okay, Stuey. I'll speak with Dr. Stienworth today. I think he said Becky gets home from college next week. You know, she's on track to receive her bachelor's degree in pre-med in three years! I wish you were that ambitious!" his mother said.

Stuart Blumenfeld was standing dead still in the upstairs hallway half way between his bedroom and the bath. He hadn't heard a word his mother said. Stuart was recalling the *incident* from last summer when Becky's swimsuit top came undone as she pulled herself up and out of their swimming pool. Just as she'd gotten one knee and both hands on the pool edge and thrust herself up and out of the water, her bikini top unsnapped and burst off, revealing two absolutely perfect, huge boobs. Her top landed on the pool rail and Becky was so surprised she let herself fall back in the water. "Stuey! Don't look! Throw me my top, please!" He'd stood staring down at Becky's breasts that were sort of *floating* in the water. "STUEY! MY TOP!" *Best day of my miserable life.*

"STUEY, I'M TALKING TO YOU! Are you listening to me? You haven't heard a word I said! I'll ask Dr. Stienworth to have Becky call you about tutoring you in chemistry when she gets home! ARE YOU LISTENING?"

Flash: "Okay, Mother."

Two days later Becky Stienworth called Stuart from college. "Hi, Stuey! This is Becky Stienworth! Remember me? Your mother says you could use some help with chemistry, but I can't tutor you. I've decided to take the summer off and be a counselor up at Camp Idlewilde! Won't that be fun? You went there once, didn't you? Great lake for swimming, huh?"

At the mention of *swimming* Stuart's mind, of course, focused on the *incident*. He was lost in memory of Becky's beautiful boobs. *Best day of my miserable life.*

"STUEY, I'M TALKING TO YOU! Are you listening to me? I asked if you went to Idlewilde!"

"Uh, yeah, I was there for two summers. Why are you going there?" Stuart asked.

"TO BE A COUNSELOR! Stuey, are you okay?"

"Yeah, sure."

"HEY! I've got a great idea! Why don't you come to camp again this year and I can tutor you at night! Wouldn't that be fun?" Becky said.

"At night? You mean after the campfire?" Stuart got an instant erection just thinking of Becky bathed in firelight. "Just you and me?"

"Of course, silly! No one else needs chemistry help."

Two days later Stuart purposefully miss-answered half the questions on his final chemistry exam, lowering his final grade to "D."

"MY GOD, STUART! How could you do so poorly? You know even one D could keep you out of the right college! AND MEDICAL SCHOOL! WHAT HAPPENED?"

Flash: "Gosh, Mom, chemistry is just so hard for me! All those symbols are confusing and I don't really understand mixing! I'm sorry."

"Did Becky Stienworth ever call you? We've got to get you some help! NOW!"

Flash: "Yeah, Mom, she called a couple of days ago, but she can't do it. She's going to spend all summer at Camp Idlewilde as a girl's counselor. Maybe we can find somebody else."

"She's the best tutor you ever had! You're going to camp again, mister! You are going to spend every available minute ALL SUMMER with Becky, studying! Now don't start whining about going to camp! I know you don't like it, but this is IMPORTANT! I'm enrolling you in Idlewilde right now! For the whole summer!"

Flash: "Aw Mom."

Dr. Ross-Blumenfeld arranged it so that she personally drove both Becky and Stuart to camp, together. All the way there she pleaded with Becky to get Stuey *back on track* in chemistry. "I just don't know what happened to him! He was doing so well and then he failed the final exam! I'm so afraid it'll keep him out of the right schools!"

"Gosh, Stuey! I didn't know you failed the final! What happened?" Becky asked.

Flash: "Don't know. Chemistry is just hard for me," Stuart said.

"Well, I'll get you straightened out, mister! I'm gonna work your buns off all summer. We'll spend every available minute on chemistry," Becky assured Dr. Ross-Blumenfeld.

Stuart spent a perfect summer under Becky's spell.

Forty years later as Dr. Stuart Blumenfeld related his story to me, the obvious question was asked. "So, how'd you do with Becky? Ever make any progress?"

"Actually, no. But I met a girl named Sarah and finally got laid the last week of camp," Dr. Blumenfeld said. "Sarah only lived about 20 miles from where I lived. She helped me get rid of my acne!"

"Did you ever confess to your mother about manipulating a summer at Idlewilde?"

"I'm a psychiatrist, not a masochist!" Stuart said.

LYING TO MIKE'S BEST FRIEND'S BIG SISTER

Freshman year of high school is often a time of extreme discomfort for boys as their daily exposure to slightly older girls provides a dizzying distraction. In eighth grade, a few of their female classmates were beginning to mature with protruding breasts and rounding backsides, but many junior and senior high school girls have full-fledged female physical attributes.

Whether sharing a drink after work or finishing a round of golf at the clubhouse tavern, the glory days of high school are often recalled and discussed by men of all ages. Many express a still-lingering, haunting humiliation as they describe trying to be *cool* and *score*. Virtually all men admit to telling any and every type of lie to accomplish their only true objective; to get laid.

Dozens of versions of men's freshman frustrations have been recounted to me, but a few stand out as classical representations of male teenage trauma, and deceit.

Mike Roush was the largest, strongest, and cockiest player on the freshman football squad. Fifteen years old, he stood 6 feet 3 and weighed 210 pounds. Both his parents were large, athletic people, and they encouraged Mike to train and condition from the time he was six years old. With above average looks and intelligence, Mike was that standout freshman kid who looked like a senior, and tried to act like one.

Mike's best friend since kindergarten, Pete Riley, never really experienced a growth spurt. Pete was still only 5 feet 5 inches tall and weighed 130 pounds. Their friends called them the "odd pair" or "too tall and too short," which pleased Mike, but made Pete mad as hell. Pete, however, was by far the smartest kid in their class. He always manipulated his classmates to do things his way.

After the third freshman football game Mike was moved up to the varsity squad. He and Pete were sitting at McDonald's discussing football and girls.

"Think you'll get to play in a varsity game, or will they just work your butt off in practice?" Pete asked.

"Coach says I'll get in a few games if conditions allow. I'm faster than either starting defensive end," Mike said.

"Yeah, but you're not stronger! Ken Stark benches 350. And he dates Katy Billings. Now that's something to strive for, to hell with football!" Pete told his friend.

"Yeah, she's hot! How big you think those boobs are?" Mike asked.

"Guess who I'm taking to the game Friday night? How about Sherry Riggs?" Pete bragged.

"Bullshit! You are not! She's like the hottest sophomore girl! Are you, really?"

"Yep, and she's driving! While you're sweating your ass off, I'll be makin' my moves!" Pete said.

"What'd you tell your mom? I thought she said you couldn't go out with older girls, asshole," Mike said.

"My folks are out of town all weekend! Jenny's supposed to be keeping an eye on me, but you know I can con her!"

Jenny was Pete's older sister. She was a freshman at a community college and Mike had been absolutely in love with her for as long as he could remember. Of course, Mike couldn't tell Pete that.

Following the game Friday night, Mike went to Pete's house and knocked on the door.

Flash: "Oh, hi, Jenny. Is Pete home?"

"Well, hello, Mike! Actually, Pete told me he was going out with you after the game. Or did I misunderstand my brother?" Jenny asked.

Mike knew there was a possibility that Pete had used him as his cover to date Sherry Riggs, but that was Pete's problem.

Flash: "Yeah, we were supposed to meet, but I couldn't find him. Bet he'll be here any minute. Can I just hang around and wait?"

"Mike, do I look stupid to you? Do think I'm as gullible as girls your age? Come on! Pete's out trying to get laid with some sophomore hottie, and I'll bet you know that! You came here to see if I was home, didn't you?"

Mike felt his knees buckle with fright. Jenny was way ahead of him. *Now what?*

"Don't stand there trying to come up with another lie, come on in," Jenny said. "Do you want a beer or anything?"

Mike couldn't respond. Despite his powerful desire for his best friend's older sister, Mike just stood there, confused and scared.

Flash: "I-I-I'm not sure I should. I mean you're... I think..."

Jenny started laughing. "Look, Mike, I'm not a child and I'm not naïve. You've been getting a hard on every time you see me for three or four years now. Come in, have one beer and talk to me." Jenny took Mike's hand and pulled him through the front door.

"Relax, Mikey. I don't bite you unless, of course, you want me to," Jenny teased. "SIT DOWN, for Christ's sake."

Mike sat. Jenny brought two Budweisers and sat opposite him. "You're still sweating from the game, or am I making you hot? Take a sip. It won't kill you. Try to unwind. Here's the deal, Mikey. You want me so bad you're speechless, but you don't have a clue what to do, right? Sit back. I'm going to show you, just for fun."

OH, MY GOD!

Two hours later, Jenny sent Mike home, forever a changed man. He walked in his front door just before midnight, his curfew.

"Hi, honey! We looked for you after the game, but we figured you went with Pete! Maybe you'll get in the game next week. Dad's already in bed. Are you alright?" Mike's mom asked. "You look a little pale."

Flash: "Pete and I and some of the guys got a burger, Mom. I'm beat. I'm gonna head on up, okay? See you in the morning."

"You didn't happen to see Jenny, did you? I would have thought she'd have to drive Pete to the game, what with their parents out of town," his mom said.

At the mention of Jenny's name Mike missed a step and nearly fell.

Flash: "No, Mom! Haven't seen her in months! Good night."

Mike lay in bed wandering if he'd ever be able to tell his mom the truth again. Or look Pete in the eye.

More than thirty-five years after losing his virginity to his best friend's older sister, Mike told me that he was still bothered that he had deceived Pete. He never mentioned lying to his mother as an issue.

At age fifty, Mike recalled that Jenny was the first female to whom he'd had that *First Flash Reaction*, way back when he was eleven or twelve. The night Mike finally got up the courage to knock on Jenny's door remained one of Mike's most vivid memories, and proudest achievements.

I WILL NOT EVER DO THAT AGAIN!

Many men remember believing that when they reached age sixteen, they'd be *grown up*. Perhaps it was reaching the legal driving age or no longer being a *freaky freshmen,* but turning sixteen seems to be the birthday most remembered by a lot of men. Leading up to that much anticipated day, boys often experiment with tobacco and alcohol because they feel they are *almost grown* and *can handle it.*

Randy Johnson lay on his bed looking at the Chicago Cubs calendar on the wall. His dad had taken him to the opening day game in April where he received the Cubs schedule on a poster-sized home/away display with *World Series Week* shown in October. But Randy was staring only at August 27th, an away game against the Dodgers, and his sixteenth birthday, just three weeks away!

He'd been taking drivers' training classes at high school and hoped his folks would let him take the test right on the 27th. *Twenty more days and I can drive! I'm grown-up! Man, I want to be able to ask Cindy for a date and not have to depend on Mom or Dad for transportation! I'm a MAN!*

"Randy, phone's for you! I think it's Mike!" his father called from downstairs.

"Hey, Mike. What's up?"

"Can you get out tonight? Harmon's folks are going out and he says Judy, Sue and Cindy are gonna stop by. Sue just got her license, so they'll be in a party mood!" Mike said.

"Yeah, my folks are going out, too, so no problem. But I need to be back before them," Randy told his best friend. "See you tonight."

Flash: "Hey, Mom. I'm gonna walk over to Dave Harmon's house and watch the game tonight with him and Mike, okay?" No mention of Judy, Sue, and Cindy.

"Okay, honey, just don't be out too late. Want us to pick you up on our way home?"

"No, Mom. That's okay. It's only five blocks. I'll be fine," Randy told his mom.

Randy jumped in the shower, washed his hair, and put on his best jeans. As soon as his folks left, he borrowed some of his father's cologne and generously splashed it all over himself. At seven o'clock, he walked to Harmon's house where Mike and Dave were waiting for him.

"Shit, Randy, you smell like a perfume counter," Mike said.

"He's just trying to impress Cindy big-tits," Dave laughed.

"Watch it! This may be your house, but I can still kick your ass, Davie boy! You just wish Sue's tits were as big as Cindy's!"

74

"I'm an ass man myself, Rando! Sue's got the best buns in the whole school," Dave said.

"You can't argue with that one, Rando! Maybe we can get these girls to play some strip poker! What do you think?" Mike always had a plan.

"Worth a try! How late will your parents be out, ass man?"

"Pretty late. They're with the Glenn's, which means they'll probably come home late and smashed!"

"Hey, here come the girls! Be cool," Mike advised.

"Hi, guys! Look what we got!" Sue said. Cindy unwrapped a half gallon bottle of sloe gin...

"What's that?" Randy asked.

"It's just the yummiest stuff you ever tasted! Sort of like a thick cherry coke with a lemon," Judy said. "But it tastes even better with a little of this mixed in!" Judy removed a fifth of vodka from her brown bag.

"WOW! Where'd you guys get all that?"

"Our secret! If we told you we'd have to kill you!" Cindy said. "So what are we gonna do? Play strip poker?"

All three boys stuttered in their haste to agree. "Y-Y-Yes!"

"Okay, but first let's have a little drinky-poo! Everybody but Sue 'cause she's driving! We brought these plastic cups so we can throw 'em away!"

Cindy filled five plastic cups with ice and then poured two fingers of the slow gin in each glass. "My mom puts a shot of vodka in her sloe gins, so here goes! Everybody take a taste!"

None of the three boys had ever tasted alcohol. Judy said she'd had wine before and Sue wasn't tasting. Cindy was the self-proclaimed expert. "To Deerfield High!"

The five teenagers tried to act as though they liked the concoction.

Flash: "Wow! That's pretty good," Mike said. *"Doesn't taste strong at all."*

Flash: "I can't taste any alcohol at all! You sure this is the real stuff?" Randy asked the girls.

"Oh, yeah!" Judy and Cindy said.

Sue lit a cigarette and watched her friends. "Let me have just one little sip of yours, Davie."

"Careful, Susan!" Judy said. "We're depending on you to drive us home!"

The six teenagers sat down in the Harmon's living room floor. "Who knows how to play strip poker?" Cindy asked.

"It's easy! We all pull a card from the deck and whoever has the lowest card has to take off one piece of clothing in each round! Whoever gets naked first loses," Mike said.

"That's NOT FAIR! We've already got our shoes off, but you guys don't! Take off your shoes so we all start even," Cindy directed. "And whoever loses each round has to take a drink!"

The first round Randy drew the two of clubs and had to remove his T-shirt. "Rats! Pour me another drink, Cindy. I finished the first one already."

By round eight, Randy was down to his jockey shorts and asked for his fourth drink.

"Uh, Rando, old buddy, better get lucky or take smaller drinks! You're starting to talk funny," Davie said.

Flash: "BULLSHIT! I'm fine! Now I'm gonna show you guys how to play this game!" Randy took a sip and drew the jack of diamonds. "SEE! You're not all gonna beat that!"

Sue drew the queen of diamonds, Judy drew an ace, and Mike and Dave drew kings. The kids were laughing so hard Cindy could barely pull a card, but she said, "One from the middle!"

It was the queen of spades. Now Randy's five friends roared with laughter. "You lost with a jack! Must not be your lucky night!" Cindy said.

"Take it off! Take it off!" Sue and Judy teased.

Randy was feeling a little strange, but he took another glass of Cindy's potion and said, "You guys have been cheating me! Somebody stooked the deck!"

When Randy pronounced *stacked* as *stooked*, his friends literally rolled in the floor, nearly hysterical with laughter.

"I'll shoooo you guys," Randy slurred.

"You mean you'll SHOW us, Randy?"

Randy downed the remainder of his fifth drink and attempted to stand up. Instead, he pitched forward right into Cindy's arms, out cold.

"Oh, Christ! Randy's really DRUNK! I thought he was teasing! What are we gonna do?" Dave asked.

"Don't know about you guys, but us girls are going to get the hell out of here! Come on. Let's go!" Cindy and Judy followed Sue to her mom's car, leaving Mike and Dave staring wide-eyed at their passed out buddy, in his jockey shorts.

"Christ! What are we gonna do? Randy's parents will kill him! And us! CHRIST!"

"Dave, calm down! Gather up the booze and the cups! Help me get Randy's clothes on him! We're gonna ditch the booze and carry Randy home and put him in his bed! Quick! Before his parents get home!" Mike had barely tasted the liquor; he was still capable of scheming.

Mike took Randy's shoulders and Dave grabbed his legs. They tied his tennis shoes together and to Randy's belt. Twenty minutes later the two boys had carried their friend the five blocks back to his house. "Quick, find his key! We gotta get him upstairs before his folks get home! And we gotta get the hell out of here!"

Getting Randy up the stairs to his bedroom was their biggest challenge, but they finally got Randy back down to his shorts and in his bed. "HURRY! HURRY! I think I hear a car!"

Mike and Dave just made it out Randy's back door as his parents' headlights illuminated the driveway. "DUCK! DUCK! Go behind the garage! Run; don't let 'em see us!"

"Go home and make sure we didn't leave any evidence in your living room, Dave! Christ, what a screw up!"

"Is Randy gonna be okay?" Dave asked.

"Who the hell knows? He must have drank half that booze! Now go, before we all get in trouble!"

"Madge, did you leave the back door unlocked?" Randy's father asked his mother.

"I don't think so. Maybe Randy's home already and forgot to lock it."

Upstairs, Randy's mom peeked in his door. "Son, are you asleep?" she softly asked.

No response.

"He's out like a light. Do you smell anything strange, Madge?" Randy's father asked.

"Yes, I do! It smells like a boat load of your Old Spice aftershave lotion!"

Randy's dad smiled. "Guess our son's starting to grow up. He'll be sixteen and driving in three weeks! Now he's using my aftershave."

Randy's parents went to bed. Two hours later they were awakened to laughter and singing. "What's that? Clock radio?"

"Dunno! It sounds like it's coming from Randy's room. Stay in bed, I'll check it out," Mr. Johnson said.

As he approached his son's room, that unusual smell became more pronounced. Randy Johnson was sitting up in his bed, singing very loudly, "Still got my shorts! I'm winning now! Winning NOW! Oh, hell yes! I'm winning now!"

"RANDY JOHNSON! What is wrong with you?"

"ZAT YOU, DAD? Pull a card, see what ya get!"

Holy shit! My son's drunk as a monkey! Can't let his mother see this! "Randy, SHUT UP! NOW! I don't want your mother to see you like this!"

But it was too late. Randy's mother had followed her husband into their son's room. "OH, MY GOD! HE'S DRUNK! OUR SON IS DRUNK!"

"HEY! HI, MOM! WANNA PLAY? JUST DRAW A CARD AND TAKE OFF YOUR CLOTHES!" Randy told her.

"Wilma, get out of the way!" Randy's father said. He hoisted his son up off his bed and threw him over his shoulder. The bathroom was only steps away.

"Where goin' Dad?" Randy slurred. His father sat him down in the bathroom floor with Randy's head nearly in the commode. Mr. Johnson popped two Alka-Seltzer tablets in a glass of water and said, "OPEN UP!"

"HUH?"

The "huh" was all that his father needed. He poured the fizzing mixture into his son's mouth causing immediate, violent heaving. Randy wreathed in convulsions, ridding his body of the poisonous mixture.

"HE'S BLEEDING, TOM! HE'S THROWING UP BLOOD!" Mrs. Johnson said.

"Relax. That's not blood. That's sloe gin. Once it's all out of him, he'll be okay. Until I beat the crap out of him when he sobers up!"

Fifteen minutes later Randy had expelled everything he'd consumed in the last twenty-four hours. Exhausted and still woozy, he was vaguely aware of his father sponging him off with cold water. Randy was shaking and freezing, imagining he was at the North Pole, when his father laid him back in his bed. After the fourth blanket was tucked around him, Randy fell into a deep and troubled sleep. *Was that his mother he heard crying?*

Nine hours later Randy awoke. Actually, his eyes opened, but he couldn't begin to move his head. *What happened? Where am I? I'M HOME! OH, SHIT!*

"Well, well! Look what the cat drug in!" Randy's father stood over his son, staring intently in his face. "Keep very quiet, mister! Your mother finally fell asleep an hour ago after watching over you all night. If you wake her up, I'm gonna kick your ass! Now, listen up! Don't even think of bull-shitting me! Where were you, really, and what did you drink?"

"Dad, I-I," Randy started.

"Careful, mister! That sounds like the beginnings of a line of crap! Straight, no-bullshit answers!"

"Dave Harmon's, Mike was there. Some girls we know brought something called sloe gin. It tasted like cherry soda. We played strip poker. Had to drink-up when you lost a hand. I lost nearly every time. Passed out. Don't remember coming home. Sort of remember you and me in our bathroom. Did I throw up?"

"You did. You drank enough to kill yourself, you idiot. Right now, I'm too mad to look at you anymore. I'm gonna go make myself some coffee and think about this. Other than to go to the bathroom, do not leave this room. Get it?"

"Yes, sir. Dad, did Mom see everything?"

"She did. Now shut-up and lay still 'til I return."

Oh, shit! How am I gonna face Mom? What can I tell her? What can I do?

Worried as he was about facing his mother, Randy Johnson fell into a deep sleep for another three hours. When he awoke this time his mother was sitting in a chair watching him.

What can I tell her? What can I do? "Uh, hi, Mom."

"Your father told me you'd explain everything! He's so upset with you he went to hit golf balls! Now talk, mister."

"Uh, what did Dad tell you?" Randy asked.

"Oh, no. You tell me what happened. Right now! You scared me to death! I thought you were going to die!" A tear rolled down his mother's cheek.

Flash: "Mom, PLEASE don't cry! I'm sorry! I really don't know what happened. I tried some weird drink at Dave's house and it just made me immediately drunk. Really. I'm sorry, Mom."

"One drink made you that drunk? And sick? You scared us to death! Your father knew to make you throw up! I think it saved your life! Why, oh why, did you do it?"

Flash: "I don't know, Mom! I won't ever taste alcohol again! I swear! I thought I was gonna die I was so sick!" As Randy's lies to his mother spewed from his lips he wondered why he was telling her something so different from what he told his father. Would his parents consult about what he told them? What would his father do if he found out Randy lied to his mother? Would his head ever stop throbbing?

"Do you solemnly swear to never drink again? Ever?" his mother asked.

Flash: "Mom, nothing could ever make me even taste liquor again! I promise!"

Randy Johnson's punishment for his night of drinking was to make him wait six months to take his driver's exam. Additionally, his father explained to him that he was on his *watch list.*

"Dad, thanks for not telling Mom everything I told you about what happened."

"We don't need to cause your mother any more pain, young man. Your behavior that night hurt her enough."

Randy Johnston's story is typical of dozens of incidents men reported in which their fathers reinforced less than full disclosure of troubling incidents from son to mother, even as they demanded to be told the entire truth themselves.

As young men learn to lie to their mothers about embarrassing situations, their fathers nearly always reinforce the need to *keep it from Mom* so she *won't be hurt.* The son's Overt and Borderline Lies to their mothers are *justified* by the Silent Lies of their fathers.

"The lie is a condition of life."

Friedrich Nietzsche

PHASE III
AGES 16-21
LYING PERFECTION

LIES TO MOM, *NOT DAD*

As frustrating and confusing as the early teen years are for a young man, nothing can prepare him for the change in his life brought about by his first real sexual experience. Between years one and fifteen he has learned to lie about almost every aspect concerning his sexuality. During Phase III, lying will take on a whole new meaning as he finds himself saying virtually anything to achieve intercourse.

It is during this phase of a man's life that the relatively innocent fibbing of youth turns into the more serious form of lying that is the subject of *Why Men Must Lie.*

Beginning in the later stages of Phase I and becoming entrenched during Phase II, males begin to understand that the sexual drive that motivates their every thought and action is not shared by the women they find so desirable. In fact, most girls seem to be relatively uninterested in what is all-pervasive to the young man—an initial sexual experience.

This is particularly exasperating for the men as their bodies mature and they leave behind the simple pleasures of boyhood in pursuit of that all important *first time*. Young men relieve their sexual desires by substituting football, ice hockey and soccer. Any sport or activity that provides an outlet for their real need can become a substitute obsession.

Less physically oriented young men may become computer geeks or video game junkies during this phase, but their sexual obsession is no less intense than their more athletic pals.

No matter what the young man appears to be involved in, his head never really clears of sexual thoughts. It is simply impossible to exaggerate a young man's sexual obsession as he seeks his first sexual partner.

When his father asked him what he wanted for his sixteenth birthday, Billy had only two wishes.

"Dad, all I want is to be able to take my driver's test on my birthday. I've taken Driver's Ed in school and you've been letting me practice parking for weeks. All I want for my birthday is to get my license that day. Oh, yeah, one more thing. Would you and Mom please quit calling me Billy? It sounds like I'm still a little boy, Dad. Please just call me Bill."

On his sixteenth birthday Bill and his dad were at the Driver's Examination Department waiting for it to open at 9:00 am. They had the first examination appointment of the morning and both father and son were excited.

"Well, son, this is a really big day! I remember getting my license just like it was yesterday. Almost nothing changes your life like being able to drive. But you've gotta be really careful, son. It would break our hearts if you injured yourself in an accident."

"Dad, what did you mean *almost* nothing changes your life like being able to drive? What could be better than driving?" Bill asked.

His father looked at watch, hoping the Driver's Examination Department would open right then, but it was still only 8:47 am.

"Well, I mean starting to drive is like the biggest day of your life so far, but there'll be other days you'll remember even more when you get to be my age. That's all I meant, son."

"You mean like the first time I get laid, dad?" Bill asked.

Dad nearly choked on his last sip of coffee. "What? I meant like the day your first child is born! You know, things like that. Why, I remember the day you were born like it was yesterday! I…"

"Come on, Dad! Tell me about your first time! Was it with Mom? How old were you? What did it feel like? Did you know what to do? Where did it happen?" Bill had completely forgotten about his drivers' exam.

"Bill, stop! You gotta calm down and get ready for your test. You won't do so well if you're all excited. We'll talk right after your test, I promise."

It took all of Bill's resolve to focus on his written exam and then do the driving portion of his test with the state trooper. He almost rolled through the last stop sign, but braked just at the last moment.

"Okay, son. You did real good. Almost blew it on that last stop sign, but you caught yourself just in time. Congratulations! Wait in the reception area and I'll have them type your temporary license. Permanent one will come in the mail in about three weeks."

"Thank you, officer! I guess I was a little nervous," Bill said.

"You're welcome! Don't let any girls sit too close to you for a while. They can be a distraction." the officer said.

"Dad, I passed! I did it! Can I drive home?"

"Congratulations, son! That's great! Yeah, you can drive home if you're not too excited. Did you miss any questions?" his dad asked.

"Nope! Got a hundred! Dad, on the way home can we finish our talk, you know, about sex?"

Bill's father had hoped that a new license would distract his son from the subject he found so hard to discuss. But he knew he had put off *the talk* way too long.

"Okay, son. But if we're gonna talk about that, I'd better drive. Tell you what. Let's stop at McDonald's to celebrate. We can talk there."

Bill swallowed down two Egg McMuffins and a large juice as his dad sipped his coffee.

"Okay, son. While you were taking your driver's test I've been thinking about all those questions you asked me and, frankly, they're not easy ones to answer. I feel a little guilty that I haven't talked to you about these things before, but I'll do my best now.

"I know we've always insisted that you tell the truth about everything and that's still the best policy, but there are some things people just don't always tell the truth about. Sex is one of those things. You asked some real tough questions before, and I'm gonna answer them directly. But I need to have your word as a man, now that you're 16, that what we talk about stays between you and me, fair enough? But let me ask you first, son, have you had any experience with a girl? Don't be embarrassed, just tell me the truth."

Bill and his father were sitting in a back booth at McDonald's and no one was close to them. Bill said, "Dad, Amber lets me, you know, feel her boobs, but that's all. But I think about her all the time, even when I try not to, I just keep wandering what it would be like! Dad, I've seen pictures in Playboy and online, so I know what girls look like, but that's all. I mean, sometimes I can't even pay attention in school 'cause I'm thinking about sex all the time! Is that wrong, Dad?"

"Son, listen to what I'm going to say. I don't know if it's right or wrong, but I do know that just about every boy your age goes through exactly what you're going through right now. Society has created a lot of rules for us over the years and, of course, there's absolute right and wrong as defined in the Bible. But the fact is, son, that sexual urge, that longing for a woman that you've been experiencing for a while now, will last throughout your life. What you do with that urge will be up to you. It's probably best to put off having intercourse for as long as you can, but that's not always possible. Remember, as badly as you want to experience intercourse and all the other pleasures that come from being sexually active, there are incredibly severe consequences for having unprotected sex. And, for example, if you had sex with Amber and she got pregnant, imagine how your two lives would be affected."

"But Dad! She doesn't have to get pregnant, does she? We could use a condom or she could start taking birth control pills! I just want her so much, Dad," Bill said.

"Son, does Amber want what you want? Are you both prepared for the consequences if she gets pregnant? And is it really Amber you want, or do you just want to experience sex? Do you feel that urge just for Amber, or are you excited by every pretty girl you see?"

"I guess every pretty girl I see affects me, Dad. How old were when you first did it? Was it with Mom? Were you married? Do you still think about sex a lot?" Bill asked his father.

Bill's Father's First Time

"Son, the best way I know to talk to you about all this is to tell what I did, what it was like for me. But, Bill, this is between you and me. What I'm about to tell you could be very hurtful to your mother, and there's just no reason for you to talk to her about it.

"I met your mother when we were in college as you've heard us discuss many times. I was twenty-four and she was twenty. I'm going to talk to you about things that happened before I even met your mother, so don't confuse any of this with how your Mom and I are now.

"When I was just a little older than you are, seventeen to be exact, I decided to join the army right out of high school. Things were a bit different back then. It was pretty normal for a boy to go into the service. Fact was, a man had a pretty good chance of getting drafted into the army if he didn't join, so lots of guys just went ahead and enlisted.

"Bill, I was every bit as obsessed with sex when I was your age as you are now. I thought about making it with a girl, any girl, twenty-four hours a day, seven days a week starting around my thirteenth birthday. You know that my father died when I was ten, so I never got to have a talk with my father like we're having now, but I'm sure he was affected by women just like you and I.

"There were several girls in my high school that made me feel the way you feel about Amber. Hell, I pretty much lusted after every girl in my class! But one girl in particular, I'll call her Kathy, really got me riled up! The way she walked, her big, round boobs, everything about her drove me crazy. She was the last thing I thought of before I went to sleep at night, and the first thing I thought of when I woke up. Dreamed about her most nights! Sound familiar?

"Well, we started dating a little bit, you know, going to the movies, maybe to a dance at school, that kind of thing. All I wanted in life was to see her with her clothes off! But she wanted something very different. She wanted to know if I loved her. She wanted to know if I wanted to marry her when we graduated. Oh, she let me feel her boobs occasionally and we kissed and hugged, but that only made it worse for me. We'd start kissing and I'd get a hard on that just wouldn't go away.

"I finally got my drivers' license when I was a senior and I'd take Kathy out every time I could use the car. We'd go to parks and make out; we went to drive-in movies, any place where I thought I might get lucky and progress beyond just kissing and the occasional feel.

"I joined the army while I was in my senior year with a reporting date delayed until after graduation. And the closer we got to finishing high school, the harder it was for me to stop when Kathy said 'stop.' One night after some heavy petting as we used to call it, Kathy asked, 'Do you love me? Do you really love just me and want to spend the rest of your life with me?'

"Now, I really liked Kathy, I guess I should say I really wanted Kathy, but love? Spend the rest of my life with her? The only thing I knew for sure was that I wanted to screw her brains out, but that's not what she asked me. She wanted to know if I loved her. And if I was willing to commit to her.

"I was sitting there with my arms around her waist, smelling some kind of sweet, woman scent with an erection about to bust out of my pants. So instead of telling Kathy that what I really wanted was to rip her clothes off her and kiss every part of her body, I said, 'Of course I love you!'

"Kathy's next question was, 'And you'll come home to me after the army?'

"My answer, 'Of course I will!'

"Now son, those were two awful lies that I told Kathy. All I wanted was sex. What she really wanted was to be loved and cared for, forever. But my lies got me what I wanted. We had sex right then and there! I was so excited, so overwhelmed by the lies I had just told that I barely got inside her before my orgasm. But that didn't matter to me right then. I had finally scored! I finally knew what it was really like to make love. Or so I thought.

"For the next nine weeks, right up until I had to report to the army, Kathy and I did it anywhere and everywhere with a kind of reckless passion totally new to both of us.

"I was absolutely on top of the world! Everything was perfect! My mind and body entered a kind of blissful harmony that I could never have imagined before. I think Kathy felt it, too, although she needed to hear me reassure her that I loved all the time.

"Then came that last night before I had to board a plane to begin basic training. I'd lied to my mom that I had to report the day before. Anything to have another night with Kathy. We rented a motel room for that last night and nearly killed each with passion. Just before dawn, just before the alarm clock went off, Kathy said, 'Honey, I haven't had a period for two months now.'

"I didn't even know what she meant. 'So?' I asked.

"I guess I could be pregnant."

"HOLY SHIT, Dad!" Bill exclaimed. "What'd you do? Was she really going to have a baby? How could you go to the army?"

"Son, I was so scared I didn't know what to do, or think! Of course I had to report the next day, that morning really, but I was petrified! My *perfect* life ended with the thought of the responsibility of a baby, and maybe having to marry Kathy. But I was about three hours away from getting on that plane to Fort Dix, and that's what I did. Back then, when you first went in the army you basically were cut off from the outside world unless there was a real family emergency, so I didn't even talk to Kathy for about three weeks. And boy did that piss her off! When I was finally able to call her she said, 'If you don't care enough to call me for twenty-two days, you don't really love me!' She hung up on me! After I'd waited in line for a phone for two hours!"

"But Dad! She was pregnant, right?" Bill asked.

"Turns out, she wasn't. She'd started her period the day after I left. I only found this out about two weeks later when I finally got another chance to call her. She was all calmed down by then and wanted to *get back to normal.* But for my first six weeks in the army, the hardest time of my young life, I'd been worried sick about maybe being a father. Made me realize that what I'd wanted from Kathy was sex, nothing more. She'd wanted love and commitment, but all I truly wanted was to get laid."

"But Dad, what happened?"

"Well, son, I was in the army for three years. At first we wrote to each other, but by the time I got back from my second tour in 'Nam, it was all over. Kathy was married and had a kid. And I was a very different person from that scared young boy I'd been three years earlier," Bill's father said.

"Dad, can you please tell me more about, you know, what the sex was like? Before you thought Kathy was pregnant?"

For the next hour, Bill's father did his best to explain what he called the *mechanics of sex* to his son. Bill had dozens of questions and his father patiently talked through answers until his son asked, "What about now, Dad? Are you and Mom happy? I mean, you know, with each other? Do you still think about other women? Does it get easier as you get older?"

"Son, I love your mother. You've had enough serious talk for one day. When you're a little older we'll talk more, but for now, I hope I've explained what I can to you. Now, let's practice your driving skills on the way home."

Bill's father's first important life discussions with his son reinforced the concept the *women can't be told everything!* Consciously or not, Bill's dad indirectly told his son that he must lie to women to survive!

The majority of men who confided in me described conversations with their fathers about sex (assuming they ever talked about it at all) that were more about the father's early sexual experiences than about what to do and not to do. Virtually every confidant recalled that their fathers emphasized the different mind sets between men and women more than anything else concerning male/female relations.

No man remembered their fathers recommending open, completely candid, honest conversations with women about sex. Or anything else for that matter!

BILL'S FIRST TIME

Some version of the father-to-son discussion between Bill and his dad is relatively common in young men's lives. Conditions and timing vary, but content, particularly the *lust versus love* portion of the story, is repeated from father-to-son time and time again.

For Bill's dad, his *First Flash Reaction* to Kathy led him to tell her lies that cost both young people extraordinary pain and discomfort. Each had their own set of needs from their relationship, but Kathy described what she wanted honestly and directly. Bill's father did not.

For several days after the birthday discussion with his father, Bill experienced a diminished desire for Amber. He found himself thinking more about the consequences his dad had described than about Amber's perfect body. But that effect on Bill's mindset ended abruptly the second Saturday after he got his driver's license.

On Saturday afternoon, Bill stopped for lunch at that same McDonald's where he and his father had *the talk*. As he sat munching on his French fries, two very attractive senior girls from his high school sat down in the booth opposite him.

"Hi, Billy!" they both said.

"Uh, hi," Bill responded. He recognized Beverly, a varsity cheerleader and one of the prettiest girls in school. He was surprised they both knew his name.

As he covertly peered over the top of his Coke, Beverly's short skirt slid far enough up her legs so that Bill could see her pink panties, and a beautiful expanse of perfectly tanned thighs. He could feel his face flush as he struggled not to keep staring. Bill risked a glance at Beverly's face and found her looking directly in his eyes. She made no attempt to cover herself. Beverly cocked her head slightly to one side and gave Bill an absolutely radiant smile.

Bill's instant erection nearly split his Levis. Embarrassed and a little scared, Bill attempted to reposition himself to hide the bulge in his pants. When he got up the courage to look up at Beverly and her friend again, they were both looking under his table at him. Bill's face was redder than the ketchup on his fries.

"If you're finished eating, why don't you come talk to us," Bev's friend said. Both girls smiled wickedly.

Bill was speechless.

"Okay, then we'll come over there."

Before Bill could protest, both girls moved to his table, one on either side of him.

"This is my cousin, Brenda. She thinks you're real cute! Say 'hi' to Brenda, Billy," Beverly teased.

"Uh, hi Brenda. I've seen you in school, but we've never met," Bill stammered.

"That's because you're always following Amber Callahan around!

Maybe you should look up every now and then to see who's looking at you! We saw you here last week with your dad, but you guys looked like you were deep in conversation. What were you talking about? You seemed so serious!" Brenda said.

Now Bill felt himself starting to sweat. *Oh, my God! Did they hear our conversation? Could they possibly know what we were talking about?*

Flash: "Uh, I had just taken my drivers' test. We were sort of, you know, celebrating. Dad was telling me about Vietnam," Bill said. First lie to Beverly and Brenda.

"Your dad was in Vietnam? Wow! That's really something! What was he telling you? I've read about that war, but I've never really known anyone who was, you know, like really there! Tell us his stories!" Brenda seemed genuinely interested.

Oh shit! Now what? His dad had never really talked at all about Vietnam to him. Bill had no stories to tell!

Flash: "I shouldn't really repeat any of that stuff. You know, it's kind of guy talk," Bill said. The lies just started to flow.

"But I like guy stuff! Come on, tell us!" Brenda insisted. "Did he get shot or anything? Does he have any medals? You should be really proud of him!"

Flash: "Look, maybe next time, but right now I have to go pick up my little sister from soccer practice. Can't be late, you know!" Bill felt the sweat streaming down his back, and lies pouring forth from his mouth.

"Hey, what team does she play on? Can I go with you to pick her up? I played right up until this season, then I got, you know, too developed to keep getting knocked around. Girls play pretty rough!" As Brenda spoke, she repositioned herself slightly and pulled her shoulders back.

All Bill could do was stare at her breasts.

"Well, how about it? Want to take me with you? You can drop me off on the way home. I just live three blocks from you!"

"You know where I live? How? I mean, I've never seen you in the neighborhood!" Bill said.

"Like I said, you need to start *looking up* occasionally, sweetie! Never know what you might see!"

Flash: "Look, I better just go get sis, she'd tell my folks and I'm not supposed to be giving kids rides just yet," Bill said.

"I'm no kid, Billy! Maybe next time, then. Now you know my name!" Brenda and Beverly got up to let Bill out of the booth.

But Bill couldn't get up just yet. His erection was actually throbbing.

Flash: "I'm gonna have to go to the men's room," Bill said.

"Okay then, Billy, we'll see you later."

The following Monday Bill was walking to his math class with Amber when Brenda fell in beside them. "Hi Billy! Who's your friend?" Brenda asked.

The past Saturday at McDonald's, Brenda had known Amber's name perfectly well; now she seemed not to recognize her.

"Uh, this is Amber. Amber, this is Brenda. I met her at McDonald's Saturday."

"'Lo," Amber murmured.

"Well, hello to you Amber! What year are you in?" Brenda asked.

"Sophomore."

"Oh. Well, see you around, Billy. Be good," Brenda said.

"What the hell did she mean, 'be good?' How well do you know her, anyway?" Amber said.

It was the first time Bill had heard Amber use the word *hell.* The frown on Amber's face was also something new to him.

"Just met her two days ago. Beverly Taylor introduced us."

"And how do you know Miss Beverly Taylor?" Amber demanded.

"I don't really. She just said 'hi' to me at McDonald's! What's eating you?" Bill asked.

"Humph!" Amber walked away from Bill. Over her shoulder Amber said, "Don't tell me you don't know about Brenda! She does it with every guy in this whole school!"

"Huh? What are you talking about? I don't even really know her! Geez!"

Amber just kept walking. "See ya later!" Bill said.

Brenda does it with every guy in school? Now that was valuable information!

The following Friday night, Bill went to the football game with his buddies. Amber hadn't spoken to him since Monday. Two rows in front of him sat Brenda with three other girls.

Just before halftime, Brenda turned and looked directly at Bill. "Hi, Billy! Where's your underclassman? Not allowed out this late?"

"Whoa! She's hot," Bill's buddies said. "How do you know her?"

"Just met her at McDonald's," Bill murmured.

The home team was losing by thirty points in the fourth quarter when Brenda turned to Bill and said, "Hey, this game's over! Want to go for a ride, Billy? I've got my mom's car and I met my friends here. Let's go somewhere."

Bill's buddies were speechless. His status within their group increased about a thousand percent as Bill and Brenda left the bleachers, hand-in-hand.

"Where do you want to go?" Bill asked as they reached Brenda's mom's car.

"Sweetie, I've got a six-pack of Bud in that cooler back there, and Mom's working nights this week. We can park right in our driveway. Nobody ever comes around. Get in and hang on," Brenda advised. Brenda parked her mom's car right up next to their garage door. "Pop a Bud, sweetie! Let's party!"

"I-I-I... uh, I've never tasted beer," Bill confessed.

"Guess it's gonna be a night of firsts for you, sweetie! Crack your window just a little bit," Brenda said. She removed her sweater and unhooked her bra. "What do you think of these?"

Two hours and three beers later, Bill's life was forever changed. His entire body still tremored and his penis was raw, but he felt wonderful. "I guess you know it was my first time, huh?" Bill asked.

"Well yeah, that first time was obviously your 'first,' but you caught on fast. What did you like most, being in me, or having my lips on you?" Brenda asked.

"Both."

"Good answer, sweetie. Was it what you thought it would be? Did I please you?"

"Oh God, yes! Way better than I could have imagined! How, er, where did you learn everything?" Bill asked.

"Bad question, sweetie. Just be happy right now and don't think backwards. Does no one any good. Help me tidy up the car, then I'll drive you home. It's nearly 1:00 am."

When Brenda pulled up in front of Bill's house, the lights were still on in the living room. "Uh oh! Somebody's waiting up for you, Billy! See ya around! Call me if you want. Now scoot!"

Instead of a kiss, Brenda reached over and gave Bill's penis a firm squeeze. "So you don't forget me!"

"I'll never forget you!" Bill said. That statement was, in fact, the truth. The lies would come later.

BILL PERFECTS HIS LYING

As Bill stepped on his porch the front door opened. "Billy, you're late! We were worried sick! You were supposed to be home by midnight. Where have you been? I didn't recognize that car! Who drove you home? Bill! Have you been drinking?" Tears welled up in his mother's eyes as she began her interrogation.

Bill's father was standing just behind his mom, watching his son intently. He said nothing.

Flash: "Uh, yeah, Mom, I had one sip of Jimmy's beer, but it tasted awful! Can't seem to get the taste out of my mouth! That was Jimmy's cousin's car. We just started talking after the game at McDonald's, and all of a sudden it was real late! I'm sorry. I won't do again," Bill said.

Immediately following his first sexual experience, Bill began automatically lying to his mother. His creativity was amazing; every response to his mother's questions was untrue.

"We were sooooo worried! Neither your father nor I could even think of sleeping! You're more than an hour late! How you could you do this?" Now his mom's tears were flowing freely. Bill's father still hadn't said a word.

"Earl, tell him he's grounded! And he can't use the car for six months! Go ahead, you're his father! Tell him!" Bill's mother was nearly hysterical.

"Son, you've disappointed us. It's very late. We'll deal with all this in the morning. Now, go to your room. You look exhausted," Bill's father said.

"You're supposed to be on your shift at the hardware store by 7:30. I'll wake you at 6:30. Go!"

Bill bolted for the steps up to his room, leaving his mother and father standing in the entrance way.

"How could he do this? He's always been such a good boy. I think it's that Jimmy Smith! He's a bad influence on our Billy!"

Bill's father held his wife in his arms and said, "Now honey, don't get all upset. He's young and a little full of himself. He'll be fine. I'll talk to him as I drive him to his Saturday job. Let's get some sleep."

Bill was in bed, but he certainly was not asleep. He was consumed with thoughts of Brenda's body and what she had done to him. As he recalled her unsnapping her bra, his raw penis once again became rock-hard. He inspected himself, wondering if he would be okay. Hell! It didn't matter. It was the best day of his life! Bill dozed off wondering when he could see Brenda again. He never once thought of Amber, or that he was supposed to meet her after the game. It never even occurred to him that every answer he had given his mother had been a lie.

At 6:30 sharp, Bill's father shook him to wake him up. "Bill, wake up! Come on, get in the shower. You smell like an old saloon. Now move!"

"Ugh, Dad, I don't feel so good. Maybe I should…."

"CAN IT! Get your ass in the shower, now, mister!" His father's tone put Bill on notice; Dad was pissed!

Then last night's activities came crashing back to Bill. Was it a dream? Was Brenda just another night time fantasy? As he entered the shower his raw, swollen penis provided the answers. It was real! He had gotten laid, four times. Plus other pleasures he hadn't even dreamed of! As the warm water brought him back to reality, Bill recalled the encounter with his parents in the foyer.

Oh shit! They know I was drinking! I lied to Mom about everything! Why was Dad so quiet last night? Why is he so mad this morning? Oh Shit!

As Bill entered the kitchen, his father handed him a cup of black coffee. "Uh, Dad, you know I don't drink coffee. Can I just get a glass of juice?"

"Take the coffee! You will drink it! Get in the car now!"

Oh shit!

Bill knew better than to ask if he could drive. He got in the front passenger's seat and waited. As his father backed out of the driveway, he said, "I'm gonna ask some questions and you're gonna answer them! No bullshit like you fed your mother last night. I want straight damn answers and absolutely none of that creativity that seems to come so easily to you these days! First, who was she and how far did it go?"

"Aw, Dad, I…"

"Straight answer with no bullshit or I'll knock some straight answers out of you, get it?" Bill's father had never spoken to him like that before in his life. He had Bill's full attention, and respect.

"Now, let's start again and can the crap! Who was she and how far did it go?"

"Uh, her name is Brenda."

"Brenda what?"

"Uh, I don't really know, Dad, honest! I just met her last Saturday at Mickey D's. She's a senior, though, at my school."

"Okay. How far did it go with Miss Brenda no-name?" His father glanced at Bill, waiting for a response.

"I guess all the way."

"What'd I say about 'no bullshit?' Start talking! Now! Did you even go to the football game like you told us?"

"Yes Dad! Honest! I went with Jimmy and Ralph and Paul. Brenda was at the game, sitting right in front of us! She wanted to go for a ride!"

"Where did you get the beer?" his Dad asked.

"Uh, she had a cooler with a six-pack in her car, Dad."

"She was driving? Where'd you go?"

"Uh, her driveway."

"WHAT? Where were her parents? Where were the neighbors? Why her driveway?" Dad asked.

"She said her mom works nights. No neighbors were around. Brenda said no one would bother us there," Bill said."

"About what time did you get to this girl's driveway?"

"I guess it was a little after 10."

"And you got home at one in the morning! Okay, you've got 23 minutes before you have to punch in. We're gonna sit right here, and you're gonna tell me everything that happened. Start talking!"

Bill talked for 15 minutes during which his father never said a word.

"That's it? You used no protection? Just lost your head and went at it, huh? The beers didn't affect you?" Bill's dad asked.

"I guess not Dad. Am I in a lot of trouble?"

"That son, depends on Brenda, doesn't it? Now get your ass in there and give 'em a good morning's work. I'll pick you up when you're finished at noon. Go!"

Bill's normal tasks at the hardware store were to sweep the store rooms and help Mr. Baker restock shelves. Fairly mindless work, but Bill enjoyed seeing how things worked throughout the store. At least a half dozen times during the morning Mr. Baker had to remind Bill what he was doing.

"Bill, are you okay? You don't seem like yourself today, son," Mr. Baker said.

"Uh, sorry sir. I was out kind of late after the football game."

"Okay. But you actually look different. Guess you're just growing up. Start moving those wheelbarrows to the front of the store."

All Bill could really focus on was the sweet memory of Brenda the night before.

When his father picked him up after work, his dad's mood seemed considerably better than when he had dropped him off that morning.

"Made it through the morning okay?" his dad asked.

"Uh, yeah Dad. Mr. Baker said I seemed distracted, though."

That actually made his father smile. "I bet you were! Okay, I've been thinking about all you told me and I've got some questions. First, though, how are you feeling about what happened last night?"

"Dad, you didn't tell Mom, did you? I mean, I don't think she would understand at all! And I'm really sorry I lied about where I was and everything. Just please don't tell Mom, okay?"

"Son, here's my first tough question. Are you really sorry about what you did last night, or are you sorry you got caught, and had to tell me? Think, now, before you answer. It's a very serious question. And of course I didn't tell your mother. This is between you and me. Your turn."

Bill was so relieved that his mother didn't *know* that he blurted out,

"God! Thanks Dad! I just don't think I could face her right now if she knew! Thank you! Dad, I'm a little scarred, you know, about what Brenda and I did, but I'm not really sorry we did it. I'm sorry I lied about it and I'm sorry I hurt you and Mom, but I'm just not sorry that I finally got laid."

Bill's last few words actually brought a slight smile to his father's face. "Do you feel different today than you've ever felt before?" his father asked.

At first it seemed an odd question, but Bill could see that his dad considered it a very serious one.

"Dad, I just couldn't have imagined how great it was! I mean, Brenda made me feel so good I almost passed out. And she seemed to really like it too! She's great!"

His father actually chuckled. "Son, your life is forever changed. The fact is I'm not mad that it happened. I'm very disappointed that you so easily lied to us about it. I will expect you to never lie to me again. But you need to be careful now. I know that nothing I can say or do can stop you from seeing Brenda again if she's willing. Son, it sounds to me like Brenda has had a considerable amount of experience, so don't go falling in love with her. And don't get mad at me for what I just said. Enjoy it while it lasts. Frankly, it probably won't last all that long. And for God's sake, use condoms."

Bill was stunned by his father's words. "Dad, I don't understand. Don't you think Brenda really likes me? Does Mom look at it like you do?"

"Oh God no, Bill! Mom would react totally differently than I am reacting. You've now had your first sexual encounter, but don't think for a minute that qualifies you to understand anything about women. Not now and not ever! Son, you may find that Brenda won't even speak to you the next time she sees you, so wise up. Be careful! Starting last night your world just got really complicated. Come talk to me when you need to, but, for God's sake, don't think for a minute that your mother would understand! By the way, what about Amber? You remember her, don't you?"

In fact, Bill hadn't really thought at all about Amber. "Actually dad, Amber hasn't spoken to me since last Monday."

"Why's that? I thought you two were kind of going together."

"She saw me talking to Brenda in school and got real mad. I don't know what for," Bill told his father.

"Gee, Bill, I guess you know now! Women, even teenage girls, just have an instinct about other females. Amber probably sensed you were going to get laid before you even thought about it. Okay, here we are in front of the house. Your mom's fixed you a nice lunch. Be extra nice, keep your mouth shut about all we just talked about, and tell her one more time that you're sorry you got home late. Nothing more. Oh, you can't use the car for a while until your mother kind of, you know, forgets about last night."

Bill's father understood his son's *First Flash Reaction* to Brenda perfectly. Nearly every man that described his father's reaction to a *first time* revelation stated that *keeping it between father and son* seemed extremely important to their fathers.

Fathers' concept of honesty normally excludes forthright discussions about sexual wants, needs, and experiences between sons and mothers. Not one man who confided in me remembered their father encouraging them to be truthful with their mother about sexual experiences.

LIES THAT ARE A VERSION OF THE TRUTH

Nearly every man recalls a variation of his own first sexual experience that is similar to Bill's, but they seldom talk candidly about it with the women in their lives. Usually sometime before their twenty-first birthday, and more often than not in an unplanned, happen-chance manner similar to Bill's experience, boys become men. The most consistent feature of men's *first time* tales is that they all wound up lying about at least some aspect of it to all the other females in their lives.

Bill couldn't begin to tell his mother the truth about any facet of that first night with Brenda, and his father encouraged him to never divulge anything about it, either.

The next Monday at school, Amber was waiting for Bill before first bell. "I looked for you after the game Friday, but Jimmy said you didn't feel good and went home early. Don't we always meet as soon as I change from by band uniform?"

"Gosh, Amber, you didn't speak to me all week! I figured you were still mad at me."

"Did you get to use the car? Did you go straight home?" Amber asked.

Flash: "Yeah, Dad let me drive to the game, but Jimmy had his car too, so I just went home. Had to be at the hardware store at 7:00 Saturday morning," Bill said.

Bill lied to Amber not only about driving to the game and going home early, he even lied to her about his starting time Saturday morning at the hardware store. Why?

The answer is simple. Bill still had that *First Flash Reaction* to Amber, even though Brenda had rocked his world. Amber was still a girl who Bill wanted to have sex with, and he was willing to say virtually anything to keep that possibility open.

"I'll help you with your calculus this week if you want. You could come to my house and study. Maybe tomorrow night?" Amber seemed anxious to make up.

"Yeah, I guess that'd be okay," Bill said.

"Great! See you later, then!" Amber said.

As Bill watched Amber's backside bounce away down the hall, a voice from behind him said, "Calculus? Yuck! I thought we knew better things to do! Or are you too scared?"

Bill turned to see Brenda standing right behind him. "Hey. Didn't see you there. How are you?"

"Mom works afternoons this week, Billy. I got an 'A' in calculus last year. You know I can teach things," Brenda teased. "Why don't you come to my house instead?"

Bill's answer was immediate, "Okay. What time?"

"Any time after three, sweetie. There'll be no one home, but little ole me. Bring a six-pack," she instructed.

Holy shit! And on a week night!

After school that day Bill caught up with Amber just before band practice.

Flash: "Hey, I forgot. I've got a chance to work an afternoon shift at the hardware store tomorrow. Maybe we could get together later in the week? Maybe Thursday?"

"Well, how late will you be working? I thought the store closed at 6:00 pm."

Flash: "Actually, I'm gonna help Mr. Baker move a couple of the displays to make room for Christmas stuff. It could take several hours," Bill said. It didn't even occur to him that Amber might walk by the store to wave at him through the window as he "got ready for Christmas." All Bill could think about was a chance to do it again with Brenda, maybe even on a comfortable couch this time.

Bill's lies to Amber came as natural as his breathing.

"Oh. Okay. Later in the week will be fine. See you tomorrow in math class."

Now Bill had two immediate problems. How to procure a six-pack of beer, and how to get himself and the beer to Brenda's house—on a school night, no less. He knew their neighbor kept several six-packs in the garage next door, but the door was usually locked. Male creativity kicked right in.

That evening, before his father got home from work, Bill asked his mother.

Flash: "Can I borrow your car after school tomorrow? I've got a chance to work an afternoon shift at the hardware store. Then I need to stay at the library and do all the research for my history project. Probably have to stay 'til it closes, I've got so much stuff to look up."

Bill launched off the lie he had told Amber about an *afternoon work shift* and then expanded the fib to *time at the library*. He was envisioning an afternoon and evening of passion with Brenda. No consequence in the world could have dissuaded Bill from lying to his mother in pursuit of more sex with Brenda.

"Well, I guess that'd be okay, but what will you do for supper? I could pack you a sandwich," his mother suggested.

A momentary pang of guilt ran through Bill's mind as his mother's kindness and generosity gave him pause. But then Bill thought about Brenda's fantastic boobs.

Flash: "Gee, Mom, that's really nice, but I'll just grab a burger if that's okay. I've got so much research to do!"

102

"Well, okay, Dear, but I wish you'd eat better. I'll pick you up after school and you can bring me back home. Don't be out too late, now!"

Now that Bill had experienced sex and saw the opportunity for more, any guilt he might have felt about the multitude of lies he began to tell Amber and his mother simply evaporated.

Tuesday morning as Bill waited for his father to take him to school, he tried the back door of his neighbor's garage and it was unlocked. Bill *borrowed* a six-pack of Budweiser and hid it in back of the lawnmower in his own garage.

Now he was all set. Bill had added petty theft to the multitude of lies he'd told to spend more time with Brenda, but it didn't really matter to him. His drive to experience more sex with a willing partner obliterated Bill's sense of right and wrong. In this phase of Bill's life, his sexual drive dominated his existence.

Interesting story, but not realistic? It is absolutely true and accurate in every detail. An anomaly? Something that happens to only one in a thousand young men? Again, no, it is perfectly representative of the transformation that occurs once a boy experiences sex.

Although the young man's life may continue to seem perfectly normal to the people around him, a profound transformation has taken place. He is beginning to understand his *First Flash Reaction* to women. The more attracted he is to the woman, the more he is affected by an undeniable wondering of what it would be like to have sex with her. His *First Flash Reaction* is not uncontrollable nor is it necessarily obvious to others.

It does, however, *happen every time he encounters a woman for the rest of his life.*

■

The *First Flash Reaction* is positive or negative, never neutral. The age of the female is of less importance in the *First Flash Reaction* men experience than what they commonly describe as a woman's animal magnetism. If the woman is shapely and pretty, she inspires a strong desire for sexual interaction in the male. Conversely, if the woman is overweight and unkempt, most males experience a distinct *avoidance reaction* that is almost as compelling as is the positive reaction to an attractive female.

What is important to understand is that this *First Flash Reaction* happens every time a mature, straight male encounters a female. The result of this *First Flash Reaction* influences how the male interacts with and responds to women in every situation.

Understanding every man's *First Flash Reaction* to them enables women to deal with the realities of their male relationships.

KENNETH STRIKER, 21, IT'S JUST WHAT MEN DO

If sixteen is the first significant birthday many men like to remember, turning twenty-one is the age nearly all men consider to be a milestone in their lives. *Fully grown, finally a man,* and *no longer a kid* are examples of common phrases I've heard as men described reaching the age of majority. A man can drink legally and vote in every state in the union at twenty-one. Unfortunately, it is also the age at which many men become convinced they "understand" and "can handle women."

Kenneth Striker woke up the night after his twenty-first birthday party feeling pretty darn proud of himself. Softly purring beside him was Marsha Miller, his current *number one girl.* She was a very pretty woman with a mind of her own. Kenny felt that she looked at the world like a man. Both were in their junior years of college, though they attended different schools. Kenny and Marsha had met at the Kroger's grocery store where both worked nearly full-time to support themselves as they completed their educations. Each had their own small apartment near their campuses. They had talked semi-seriously about moving in together so they could split the rent, allowing them each to reduce hours worked and enjoy their last few semesters.

"Hey, wake-up, babe! We've got to get moving! It's almost 7," Kenny said.

As Marsha rolled toward him Kenny felt her warmth and smelled that delicious woman smell that excited him so.

"How about a quickie?" Marsha teased. "You weren't exactly on top of your game last night, if you know what I mean."

"What? I was too! What do you mean?" Kenny asked.

"Well, you had just enough to drink that you were a little anxious! Then you went right to sleep while I was seeking more attention," Marsha said. "Come on, we've got time!"

"I've got to punch in at eight and traffic is rough going that direction. It won't matter if you're late to lecture, but I've gotta work. I'm going in the shower."

"Okay, but you owe me one," Marsha teased.

As Kenny drove to work, Marsha's words haunted him, "You were a little anxious! Then you went right to sleep while I was seeking more attention." *Damn! That woman's hard to satisfy. Wouldn't want to be married to her.*

After six hours stocking shelves, Kenny hurried to afternoon classes. He took the first available seat closest to the door just before the professor started speaking. As Kenny searched for a pencil, he dropped his note pad in front of the girl next to him, just out of his reach. She was so engrossed in the class she didn't notice.

"Excuse me. Would you reach my note pad, please? I dropped it right by your right foot," Kenny said in a near whisper.

No response.

"Would you reach my note pad, please?" he repeated.

Still no response. Kenny bent forward in his seat and carefully began to reach around the girl's ankles to retrieve his pad.

"If you want to play with my leg, you have to buy coffee after class," the girl whispered.

"Huh? I was ju..." Kenny stopped mid-sentence. The girl he was looking at was gorgeous, if slightly overweight. "Uh, okay."

When the lecture ended the girl said, "Hi. My name's Annie. I heard you the first time you asked about your notepad, but I just couldn't resist messing with you! You work at Kroger's down by the mall. I see you there all the time stocking shelves. Was this your last class of the afternoon?"

"I'm Kenny. Nice to meet you. No, unfortunately I have a five o'clock marketing class."

"I've got a five o'clock, too! Meet you at Demi's about 6:15? You owe me a coffee. I always collect my debts!" Annie teased.

Later at Demi's, Kenny asked, "Why haven't I noticed you around campus before? You must be at least a junior to be in that accounting lecture."

"Just returned to school last quarter. Took some time off to get my head together. Do you have a steady girl?" Annie asked.

Wow! This chick is aggressive!

Flash: "Uh, no, not really. Why?"

"Do you live by yourself?"

"Yeah. Why?"

"I'm looking for a roommate. Girls are way too difficult, plus apartments near campus are hard to find. Would you consider a woman for a roommate?" Annie asked.

Maybe too aggressive! "I only have a one bedroom," Kenny said. "Might be a little crowded."

"Can I see your apartment? I mean, if you're not too busy," Annie said.

Whoa!

Flash: "Yesterday was my birthday and I had a little party over there. It's really pretty messy right now. Besides, I didn't say I wanted a roommate! You're a little fast, aren't you?"

"But you want me, right? I can see it in your face," Annie said.

All caution and common sense left Kenny's brain. *Marsha's working tonight and then she's gonna be studying. I can handle this! Maybe I can score with Annie! She's got a hell of a body! Marsha never has to know!*

"You really want to see my apartment? Right now?"

"You don't have a steady girl, right? Sure, I'd like to see your apartment! Let's go. I've got my car, so I'll follow you."

Now Striker was feeling really cocky! *Turning twenty-one is working out pretty damn well even if Marsha said I wasn't all that good last night! I'll show her!*

As Kenny opened his apartment door, his phone was ringing. "Make yourself at home, Annie. I'll just grab that phone and then show you around," Kenny said.

The phone was Marsha. "How was class?" she asked. "Anything exciting happen?"

Flash: "Nope. Just got home and I've got a ton of research to do."

"Maybe I'll see you after work tomorrow night, then. You're working 'til 10 aren't you?" Marsha asked.

"Yep. See you then. Good night," Kenny told Marsha.

"Looks like you had quite a party," Annie said. "Any alcohol left over?"

Wow! This is gonna be easy! "What do you drink?" Kenny asked.

"Whatever you've got! Okay if I take my shoes off? Can I see the bedroom? Then I need to use the bathroom, okay?"

Striker poured two vodka rocks and said, "Look around and be comfortable. After you use the ladies' room we can talk."

Annie closed the bedroom door behind her saying, "I'll just be a sec."

Boy oh boy! I'm gonna love being twenty-one! Got women coming after me on all sides! Striker took a nice long pull on his vodka.

After ten minutes, Kenny called out, "You okay in there Annie? Your vodka's waiting!"

"Be right there" Annie said.

When Annie emerged from the bedroom, she had on fresh make-up and had loosened the top two buttons on her blouse. She accepted the vodka, but sat on a chair opposite Striker. "So, you have this nice little apartment and no girlfriend to share it with, right? You're not gay are you?"

"Hell no! Would I have invited you over if I was gay? Tell me a little about yourself. Why did you take time off school? What are you majoring in?"

"Criminal justice. I could be done in three semesters if I applied myself. Whose sweater is that on the floor on the other side of the bed?" Annie casually asked.

Oh shit! How did I miss that? Marsha must've left that damn blue sweater she wears at work all the time!

Flash: "Uh, if it's blue it's mine," Kenny tried.

"Really? Looks pretty feminine to me. Hey, if you've got a girlfriend that's cool. No need to lie about it. We just met, after all," Annie said.

Flash: "I know that. I don't have a girlfriend. Maybe someone from the party last night left it."

"Actually, it looks just like the sweater my friend Marsha wears to work all the time. You must know her, she works at the same place where you work."

Oh shit!

Flash: "Uh, I know who she is, that's all."

At that moment there was a knock on Kenny's door, followed by, "Hey

Kenny, honey, are you in there? I think I left my sweater by the bed."

Shit! God damn hell! How can this be happening! "Uh, hold on," Kenny said.

"You know, that sounds like Marsha's voice," Annie said. Before Striker could get his wits about him, Annie jumped up and opened the door.

"Well, look who's here!" Marsha said. "If it isn't my old friend Annie! I didn't know you two knew each other!"

Flash: "Uh, I just met Annie in class today. We were gonna study…" Kenny realized he'd been set up.

Marsha and Annie both started laughing! "Just like you said, girlfriend! He denied he was dating anyone and couldn't wait to get me over here. Kenny-boy took the roommate bait like a mouse eatin' cheese! Gave him every chance to fess up, but he was seriously on the make! Guess you're instinct's were right-on, Marsha!"

"I'll buy you a beer, Annie. Thanks for helping me see through this liar!" Marsha said. "Striker, don't even speak to me when you see me at work! Now get me my sweater!"

Kenny Striker sat and contemplated what had just happened. What could he have done differently? Been more careful? Been less aggressive? Try to find one girl he could settle in with for a while?

The fact was, at age twenty-one, Kenny Striker's *First Flash Reaction* to women ruled his existence. Nearly every confidant I listened to admitted to being completely driven by his sexual appetite at the end of Phase III.

"Half the truth is often a great lie."

Benjamin Franklin

PHASE IV
AGES 22-35
BALANCING LYING AND LIFE

CHARLIE JONES, 23, MARRIED MEANS MORE LIES

Once men enjoy their first sexual contact, the drive to expand their experience to as many other females as possible begins. This drive is as basic as breathing for all heterosexual males. It is *why men must lie to women.*

There are some men who, despite continuing to experience the *First Flash Reaction*, never act on their desire for multiple female partners. After listening to hundreds of men describe their sexual practices and desires, however, I believe this to be an extremely small percentage of the male population. This small minority experiences the *First Flash Reaction* to women, but usually concedes that their fidelity is due to fear of reprisal or lack of opportunity, rather than to absence of desire.

Charlie Jones awoke on the morning of his twenty-third birthday feeling elated and terrified. Today was Charlie's wedding day. His fiancée,

Linda, was one of the most gorgeous creatures on earth. All of Charlie's buddies said he was lucky as hell to have found a girl who was not only beautiful, but intelligent, sensitive, and caring.

Charlie lay in bed, afraid to get up. He remembered Linda's last words to him the previous evening, just before he'd left to attend his bachelor's party.

"Now, don't even think of trying to talk me into coming back and staying here tonight. I'm at least a little old fashioned. I believe it's bad luck for the groom to see his bride before he sees her at the altar on their wedding day, so I'm staying with Sue tonight. Have a good time with your buddies, but don't get too drunk. And don't you dare let them talk you in to doing anything stupid! You know, like letting some go-go girl make you misbehave!"

How he wished he'd listened to Linda's advice. Charlie's buddies had started buying him double shots of tequila, and paying for topless beauties to do lap dances for him early the previous evening. One of the dancers, Monique, had taken a liking to him and took him home to her place for *more entertainment.* Now he was lying beside Monique, listening to her snore, afraid to move. His head pounded from a world-class hangover.

Charlie cautiously raised the sheet just enough to inspect himself and saw that his penis was raw. He couldn't see a clock, but the sun was already lighting the morning sky.

Holy shit! I'm getting married today! What the hell am I doing here?

Charlie eased himself out of Monique's bed and began searching for his clothes which were strewn all around her apartment. He found everything except one sock and got dressed up close to the front door. His head hurt so badly he could barely stay balanced to get his pants on. Charlie gently turned the door knob, hoping to silently escape without waking Monique, when he reached into a pocket for his car keys.

Oh, Christ! Where are my keys? And my wallet? Damn!

"Looking for these, cutie?" Monique asked as she provocatively leaned her naked body against the bedroom door frame, holding Charlie's keys and wallet high over her head.

"Uh, yeah. I gotta go," Charlie mumbled.

"Well, it would be kinda nice if you, you know, showed some appreciation for last evening. I was thinking a C-Note would be nice," she said.

"What? You're a working girl? I thought you liked me!"

"Look, sweetheart, if I remember correctly, today is your wedding day. I didn't bring you home because I love you, or wanted to change your mind. Your buddies said you wanted to get your *last action*, so they followed us home and left your car right out front. You were way too drunk to drive. So if you want to be on time for your big day, flush a hundred dollar bill out, and I'll trade you your keys for the cash." Monique said as she tossed him his wallet.

Charlie wanted to cry. He was angry and ashamed, but more than a little intimidated by Monique's confidence. He removed three twenties and a ten from his wallet.

Flash: "This is all I've got. Now give me my keys, please."

"Actually, cutie, there's a C-Note tucked in back of your driver's license. I'll take that! Now get the hell out of here!" Monique palmed the hundred dollar bill and threw Charlie's keys at him.

As Charlie started his car, he saw his watch suspended from the gearshift lever. Eight thirty! He was due at the church in two and a half hours! He shook his head to clear the cobwebs and tried to remember how to get back to his side of town.

When Charlie pulled up in front of his apartment his best man and two of his ushers were waiting for him.

"You look like shit, Charlie! How was Monique?" his best friend, Dennis, asked.

"Uh, okay. Look, I gotta get fixed up! I feel like my head is gonna split and we're due at the church in two hours," Charlie said.

"Relax! We picked up the tuxes and the flowers. Jump in the shower and get presentable while we put on the monkey suits. We'll make it with time to spare!"

In fact, they did make it. As Charlie stood looking toward the rear of the church awaiting the appearance of Linda and her father, his family and friends smiled their encouragement. His mother mouthed "I love you, Son" from her front row seat.

Linda made her grand entrance and the ceremony began.

"And do you, Charlie, promise to love, honor, obey and forsake all others?" the pastor asked.

Charlie looked directly at Linda and said,

Flash: "I do."

Later, as he and Linda waited for their guests to start through the reception line Linda asked, "How was your last free night? Did you have a good time? How drunk were you? You looked a little pale there at the altar!"

Christ, I hope I'm alright! What was I thinking? I must've been nuts to go with that damn dancer bitch!

Flash: "I'm good! Wasn't out that late, guess I was just a little nervous," Charlie told his new bride. Please, God, let me just get through the next few hours.

Did Charlie's behavior mean that he did not love Linda? Was his *last night of freedom* atypical of a bachelor party? Did Charlie consider his responses to Linda's receiving line questions to be outrageous lies?

The answer to all of those questions is "no." Charlie's *First Flash Reaction* to Monique was so extreme that his judgment was overridden by sexual desire. His new wife was only the second woman with whom Charlie had ever had sex; he simply couldn't resist the bawdy dancer.

Linda and Charlie met as college freshmen and began living together their sophomore year. When Linda had asked Charlie if she was *enough for him* a few weeks prior their wedding, he answered, "Yes, dear! Come on, take it off! Let's do it!"

In fact, Charlie was attracted to lots of other women, particularly a couple of Linda's bridesmaids. He could not make himself be honest with his fiancée. Charlie believed that he knew what Linda wanted to hear. Linda was anxious to get pregnant and be a full-time mom and Charlie did not want to disappoint her. So he lied to her. What Charlie wanted was to start a career and begin climbing the corporate ladder, join a golf club and live the *good life*. That's the part of his dreams that Charlie shared with Linda.

Linda assumed that the comfortable sex she shared with Charlie was all he wanted and needed.

Charlie hadn't had sex with another woman since he'd moved in with Linda in college until his buddies fixed him up with Monique at his bachelor's party. Humiliated as he'd been when Monique asked for money, the rough, thoughtless, extremely physical sex he'd enjoyed with her contrasted quite favorably with the comfortable sex he shared with Linda.

On their wedding night Charlie *begged off* when Linda came to him in their hotel room. "I'm just too keyed up, honey. We'll make up for it in the morning." In fact, it wasn't until three days later on their honeymoon in the Bahamas that Charlie made love to his new wife.

"I was beginning to wander about you, sweetie," Linda said. "Guess the wedding had you more up tight than I realized."

Flash: "Yeah, babe, but I'm good now. Thanks for being patient with me."

Charlie's bachelor party disaster is similar to stories I heard often as men described their pre- and post-marriage emotions. Many other factors, however, cause men to experience performance problems on their wedding nights. All involve lying.

LEE FAIR, 25, MOM CAN'T KNOW

Men feel the need to lie to women about nearly everything as they mature. A common theme among my confidants was lying to their mothers about something they had promised not to do, or buy.

On Lee Fair's twenty-fifth birthday he awoke early and went directly to the Honda dealer. For as long as Lee could remember he had longed to own and ride a motorcycle. Lee's mother, however, had made him promise three things: 1. Never smoke cigarettes, 2. Never drink alcohol, and, most importantly of all, 3. Never, ever even think of riding a motorcycle.

All through his undergraduate studies and now through the first three years of medical school, Lee had abided by his mother's wishes regarding motorcycles. This was, however, the day he would finally purchase his first bike. Honda had just begun selling their first large displacement motorcycle in the US, a 750cc inline four cylinder model that promised to be the fastest, coolest bike available anywhere. Lee just had to have one.

As he stood listening to the salesman's *pitch* about the motorcycle's revolutionary design and amazing acceleration, Lee considered how he could hide his bike from his mother.

Why hide it? I'll just tell Mom that bike in back of the apartment belongs to a buddy who didn't want to leave it on the street! She'll never find out.

Right in the middle of the salesman's summation Lee said, "How much?"

"Well, my friend, you probably know these bikes are in demand! But seeing as how you're still in med school I'll let you have it for Honda's suggested retail price of $1,795. Plus tax, of course. Out the door with a plate, $1,900! We even have financing available."

Lee had done his research and knew he'd have to pay full price. "If you've got one with the black tank with gold trim I'll take it."

"How are you going to pay for it?" the salesman asked.

"Cash." Lee had been saving for three years so he could hide the purchase from his mom.

"How about a helmet and gloves? Got 'em on sale!"

"Nope! Just write up the bike," Lee said.

"Are you an experienced rider? You know you need to be really careful with these 750s. They're lightening quick."

"I've been practicing on my friend's Triumph for years. I'm ready to ride."

Shortly after noon Lee pulled out of the Honda dealer on his brand new 750. The day was clear and bright and Lee rode around town all afternoon, loving his new motorcycle. He had a date with a new girl that night, but decided he'd better not show up on his bike because he'd never carried a passenger. That would require more practice.

Lee carefully set his new pride and joy up on its center stand in the parking space behind his apartment. He was standing back admiring the bike's lines when his roommate, Jeffery, yelled out their apartment window. "Hey Lee! You're mom's on the phone and she says it's urgent!"

"Hello, Mother. How are you?"

"Denise Brinkman just called and said she saw you riding a motorcycle!

Right in front of Bernie's Deli on Main Street! She said she was sure it was you!"

Oh, shit! What are the odds of that? Denise Brinkman is the only woman my mom knows in all of Ann Arbor and she has to see me on day one?

Flash: "Come on, Mom! You know I would never ride a motorcycle! I promised!" Lee said.

"She said she was sure it was you! Don't lie to me, Lee! Were you riding a big, black Honda?"

Flash: "Of course not! What kind of bike did she say it was?"

"A Honda! Black with chrome stuff on it! And Denise said you had on a leather jacket! Black leather!"

Denise is a frigging detective! Now I'm gonna have to hide my jacket when Mom visits. Thank God she lives forty miles away!

Flash: "Mom, I don't own a leather jacket and you know it. Mrs. Brinkman made a mistake! It must have been someone who looked like me!" Lee told his mother.

"You're almost through medical school at the University of Michigan! Surely you wouldn't risk everything by riding a motorcycle! Tell me it wasn't you!"

Flash: "Mom, she made a mistake! It wasn't me. I've been studying all day. I just walked in from the library when you called!"

"You'd better not have a Honda, Lee! You promised!"

Flash: "Mom! It's fine! I have no motorcycle! Relax, Mom! I'll call you tomorrow, okay?"

"You're in the shit, now, buddy," Jeffrey said. "You can't leave it out back! Your mom will be on the lookout for any evidence of a bike!"

"I'll think of something! I was gonna have to store it through the winter anyway! Maybe I can find a garage to rent. Christ, you'd think I'd just committed murder or something!"

"Your mom will murder you when she finds out, man," Jeffrey said. "Can I take it for a spin?"

"In your dreams, asshole! I gotta get ready to meet Jen. What are you doing tonight?"

"Studying, like you should be! Are you going to try to get Jen to come back here?" Jeffrey asked.

"Sure, if I can. Don't be hanging out on the couch if you hear the door before midnight, okay?"

"Yeah sure! See you in the am."

Lee met Jen at The Earl Restaurant and Bar. They sat in the lower lounge where they could enjoy a cigarette with their drinks. After dinner, Jen agreed to go back to Lee's place to listen to Bob Dylan. Lee was hoping to get lucky with Jen. She seemed anxious to accompany him back to his apartment. *Now, if only Jeffrey will stay out my way!*

Lee carefully eased his key into the front door, hoping his roommate was in his bedroom. As he pushed the door open, cigarette in one hand and his arm around Jen, Lee dropped his keys. That woke his mother up from where she'd been napping on the couch.

"Well, hello dear! Is that a cigarette in your hand? You smell like an old saloon! And there's a black Honda motorcycle in your parking space! Who's that?" Lee's mother said, pointing at Jen.

Oh, Shit! "Hi, er, mom. This is Jen."

Lee Fair recalled that he did not, in fact, get lucky with Jen that night. His mother woke up the entire apartment complex screaming at him about all the lies he had been telling her.

"You're smoking! You've been drinking! And I know that's your motorcycle out back! How could you?" Mrs. Fair was near hysterical.

Flash: "Mom, I can explain," Lee began. Jen excused herself and literally ran out the door. Lee sat up all night trying to convince his mother that he hadn't been lying.

More than thirty years later Dr. Fair still shuddered at the memory of the night his mother found him out.

"Doc, you had to know she'd find out sooner or later. Did your mother ever forgive you?"

"Eventually, yes. But I had to be really careful after that! She still brings up that night occasionally!"

"Do you still ride motorcycles?"

"Sure, but don't tell my mom!" Dr. Fair said. "I keep my bikes at my buddy's house up north now!"

WHY MEN MUST LIE

ALAN BECKMAN, 28, LIES HIS WAY TO MISERY

Alan Beckman was on top of the world at his bachelor party as he listened to a toast from his soon-to-be father-in-law.

"Here's to you, Alan! I know my little girl and you are going to be very, very happy. I welcome you to our family and know that you'll be the son I've always wanted! And give us the grandsons we've always wanted! May you become our firm's youngest partner," William 'Win 'em All' Purcell said.

The thirty attendees gathered in the men's grill at Purcell's country club clicked their glasses and yelled, "Here, here!"

"Thank you Mr. Purcell, er, William," Alan began. He was still struggling with calling the Senior Partner of Purcell & Roberts by his first name. "I look forward to granting your wishes, sir, and your daughter's!"

The men cheered again. "May you and Connie be as happy as her mother and I!" William Purcell responded. Connie Purcell was William's only child and he doted on her constantly.

What a night! Since Alan and Connie had announced their engagement seven months ago, Alan's life had become a whirlwind of ever-increasing activity, excitement, and anxiety. A young man from the *other side of the tracks,* Alan had positioned himself quite nicely. After graduating summa cum laude from Harvard Law, Alan won a position with one of the most prestigious law firms in Boston. Now he was marrying the founding partner's daughter.

Only two years out of law school, Alan had just made junior partner at Purcell & Roberts. He had convinced himself that it was his intellect and hard work that earned him the promotion; not his upcoming marriage to Connie Purcell.

Alan and Connie's wedding the next day was the stuff of society page extravaganza. Five hundred of Boston's most prominent citizens were in attendance to help the couple celebrate. William Purcell's private jet delivered the new Mr. and Mrs. Beckman to a secluded villa on the Italian Riviera, where they would enjoy their first month of marital bliss.

"Isn't this place just perfect, honey? Wasn't the wedding simply the best? Aren't we the two luckiest people in the world?" Connie said to Alan after breakfast on the balcony overlooking the Mediterranean.

"Yes, dear, it's perfect," Alan responded.

"Let's get pregnant right now! Why wait? I stopped taking the pill three months ago, so we should be fine! Mommy and Daddy will be thrilled!" Connie's enthusiasm made her giddy.

"Uh, I thought we were going to wait a while. You didn't tell me you were off the pill. What if you're already pregnant? That could be embarrassing!"

"Why? We're married! Come on, let's try right now!" Connie was pulling Alan up and out of his chair. She started shedding her clothes on the way up the steps, revealing her perfect body on the top step.

For the first time since Alan had met Connie, he just couldn't get an erection.

"What's wrong with you?" Connie demanded. "Where's that 'I want you every minute' passion you've always had? Come on! I thought you loved me!"

Alan did love Connie. He was, however, experiencing a relatively common male reaction to the finality of the wedding ceremony, *responsibility deflation*.

Alan's *First Flash Reaction* to Connie some two years previous had been extreme. He remembered vividly his immediate erection when he'd been introduced to Connie at a welcoming function for new employees of Purcell & Roberts. He could still picture her bare shoulders and ample cleavage revealed by the cut of her pink and orange sundress.

Alan had sworn his everlasting love to Connie and promised her he would *never even look at another woman*. He'd vowed that the career advantage of being the fiancée of the senior partner's daughter was not relevant to his pursuit of her.

Alan's actions did not match his rhetoric. Throughout their engagement, every time Alan got a chance to visit his boyhood home in Pittsburgh, he spent the majority of the time having sex with Renee Sloan. Renee had been Alan's first sexual partner and he'd been sort of committed to her right up until he met Connie. Though not as beautiful and certainly not as sophisticated as Connie, Renee exuded sexuality.

Laying in that beautiful bed with Connie in the idyllic Riviera setting, all Alan could think of was how trapped he now felt. He admitted to himself for the first time that the opportunity at Purcell & Roberts was equally as important as Connie's body in his decision to marry Connie.

"Alan! What's wrong?" Connie's tone jarred Alan back to the present.

Flash: "I just love you so much and I'm so overwhelmed by your parent's generosity that I feel inadequate," Alan said. "Let me hold you for a while, I'll be okay."

"Let me help you, honey," Connie said.

Connie's lips on him brought about the desired erection. Alan made love to his new wife, but when he closed his eyes he pictured Renee Sloan.

Alan Beckman's *responsibility deflation* emotion and corresponding reaction following his wedding are not uncommon. For many men the finality of their marriage vows inhibits their sexual desire for some period of time.

When Connie surprised Alan by announcing that she'd *been off the pill* for months and wanted to get pregnant immediately, the reality of his new responsibility jarred him into facing his situation. That Connie might already be pregnant was debilitating.

Expressing his true emotions to Connie, telling her the truth, never occurred to Alan.

JOHN HEDGES, 30, LIES AWAY HIS VETTE

John and Joan Hedges had been married for five years; most of that time very happily enjoying the pleasures of two good incomes and minimal responsibility. John was a regional salesman for a pharmaceutical company and Joan had just made partner in a law firm. They planned to buy a new Corvette to celebrate Joan's achievement.

"Ready to go order our 'Vette? Still thinking of crystal red metallic with beige interior?" John asked.

"Maybe we should put that off a while," Joan said. "I think I may be pregnant."

"What? I thought we were going to wait until you got established in your practice! How did this happen? Are you sure?"

John's response was clearly not what Joan had hoped for. "I'm pretty sure, honey. We knew this could happen after I had to stop taking the pill. We weren't as careful as we said we'd be."

John sat staring into his coffee, too stunned to say anything for several minutes. Joan had always talked about starting a family, but the prospect had always been out in the future, when they were ready. John had no desire whatsoever to be a father. In fact, just the thought of parental responsibility made John cringe. John had never told Joan how he really felt.

"Honey, what's wrong? We always talked about having children, someday. I'm thirty-two! I don't want to wait any longer. We can afford it. I'll only be off work a few months," Joan explained. "Say something!"

There goes my Vette! There goes golf every weekend! Christ! Is it too late for an abortion? Sex probably won't even be the same! "When will you know for sure?" John asked.

"I'm pretty sure right now, John. Are you upset? We've always talked about having children. What's wrong?" Joan's joy vanished as she watched her husband's reaction to her news.

Flash: "I'm just surprised, that's all. What's next? When will you know if it's a boy or girl? How long can we still, you know, have sex?" John asked.

As upset as John was, he still couldn't express his true feelings to his wife.

More than half of the men who spoke candidly to me describe a reaction similar to John's when first told they were about to become fathers. This is not to say that the majority of these men don't eventually accept and shoulder the responsibility of fatherhood; most do.

On an intellectual level, men understand that sexual intercourse can lead to parenthood, but that is seldom the reason men seek sex. Time and again men remember being truly surprised, even shocked, when informed they have a child on the way.

I found that the younger men I spoke with were much more likely to be shocked by their impending fatherhood than men in Phases VI and VII, the two latter groups being comprised of men fifty-five years and older. These seniors came of age prior to extensive use of the birth control pill by their female partners. They recall fear of getting their partners pregnant as at least some deterrent to sexual intercourse. Men younger than fifty-five came of age expecting their female partners to be *on the pill;* therefore *safe* as recipients of their advances.

Over and over men said to me, "Hell! I knew she was on the pill! She wasn't gonna get pregnant! What did I care? I just wanted to get laid!"

It seems that the sexual freedom women have achieved through the advent of the birth control pill is an even greater liberator of men who now expect that women will only get pregnant when they choose to do so.

TIGER WOODS, 33, EL SUPREMO
FIRST FLASH REACTOR

Late in 2009 the world's top rated golfer and best known athlete, Tiger Woods, age thirty-three, was revealed as perhaps the best example in modern times of *Why Men Must Lie.* Woods' *First Flash Reaction* to women was so extreme that he jeopardized everything he'd achieved in pursuit of his next sexual conquest.

Although Woods appeared to have an idyllic professional and personal lifestyle, he clearly lied to his wife about his true sexual desires from the moment he met her. The elaborate web of deceit that Woods formulated to cover up what he really wanted from virtually every attractive woman he came in contact with will be analyzed and discussed for years to come by an overly zealous sports media.

World speculation centers on whether Woods is *sorry* and whether he will *change his ways.*

The information now publically available about Woods' behavior is crystal clear; Tiger's *First Flash Reaction* was severe to the extreme. Despite the multi-million dollar public relations effort underway to resurrect Woods' public image, any expectation that he will be capable of truly changing his *First Flash Reaction* to women is unrealistic. Not only did Woods lie to his wife, the transcripts of emails with his various sexual partners are clear evidence that he consistently lied to all of the women he pursued.

I *circled back* to more than one-hundred men whose stories helped formulate *Why Men Must Lie;* not one of them was at all surprised by Tiger Woods' lifestyle.

Woods' *Triple A* personality combined with unlimited affluence and therefore opportunity, made it impossible for him not to lie to women to fulfill his sexual desires. Almost all of the world-ranked professional golfers that are Woods' associates have come out in support of forgiving him and wishing him future success in his golfing career. Why?

A main reason is that the majority of world-ranked professional golfers relate to Woods' dilemma. To a lesser degree all professional athletes have the affluence and opportunity to enjoy a life-style whereby they can enjoy their *First Flash Reaction* to numerous women just like Woods did.

Woods' predicament is representative of the *First Flash Reaction* results as related to me by approximately half of the men who have candidly shared their experiences. This coincides directly with the American divorce rate of fifty percent for first marriages. The other half of men featured in *Why Men Must Lie* were able to reach some level of accommodation with their significant other that enabled the relationship to survive.

Had Tiger Woods been completely honest with his fiancée about his sexual desires prior to their marriage, would she have married him? Would any woman even consider marrying a man who candidly describes his *First Flash Reaction* personality trait to her? Does the seemingly improbable situation whereby a man honestly describes his *First Flash Reaction* to a prospective wife preclude that he will ever find a woman willing to marry him?

The answers to these three questions are less straightforward than most people expect. Many readers will find the answers counterintuitive or simply unbelievable. Real-life solutions often seem bizarre.

Asian and European men of significant affluence like Tiger Woods are sometimes partially honest with prospective wives by negotiating to discreetly keep mistresses as part of pre-nuptial contracts. A limited number of my confidants claim to have fully disclosed their *First Flash Reaction* to perspective mates because they knew it was beyond their ability to control. In these extraordinarily rare situations, approximately half of the women did agree to accept their husbands' conditions. Women who enter these types of pre-nuptial contracts normally are guaranteed significant financial security in exchange for accepting their husbands' infidelities.

The few men who have described this type of arrangement to me usually admit to exceeding the limitations of the agreements by keeping more women *on the side* than is understood within the pre-nuptial *deal.*

Affluence combined with opportunity significantly increases the odds that men will act on their *First Flash Reaction* to the women they encounter. There has been a great deal of discussion about how much Tiger Woods had to lose by behaving as he did. His potential career setbacks, the un-raveling of his lucrative sponsor endorsements, even the possible loss of his family simply were not sufficient deterrents to offset his sexual drive for multiple female conquests.

REVEREND ROGERS, 35, SWEARS ON HIS BIBLE

Reverend Daniel Rogers had been blessed with a combination of good looks, an angelic voice, and reasonable intelligence. A third-generation pastor, Rogers had never considered any career other than doing *God's work.*

He particularly enjoyed Sunday mornings when he could gaze out on his congregation and receive the adoration of his followers, especially the ladies. Daniel's wife and four young children normally sat in the first pew, center, and he often referred to his family as he delivered his weekly sermons. Occasionally, one of his son's would call out to his father or ask him a question right in the middle of his delivery. Reverend Rogers always responded to these outbursts with good humor and kindness, further endearing him to his flock.

At age thirty-five, Rogers lead one of the largest Baptist congregations in Texas, and he and his family enjoyed an affluent lifestyle.

Reverend Rogers had only one problem. Starting two years previously, he had succumbed to his *First Flash Reaction* to an attractive young widow in the church choir, Angela Brooks. They began having sex anywhere and everywhere that the opportunity presented itself, even in his rectory.

Now, Mrs. Brooks and her two children usually sat just behind his family on Sunday mornings. Rogers struggled to stay focused on his sermons. This particular Sunday, Angela had him half crazy as she unabashedly beamed her inviting smile at him.

Although Reverend Rogers had been tempted by several women in the past, he'd always been able to resist the opportunities until Mrs. Brooks made herself so available to him. So far, however, he and Mrs. Brooks had been discreet. No one suspected any connection between them, and his life continued pretty much as it had been, except that he found himself lying constantly to his wife to *cover* his time with Mrs. Brooks.

Flash: "Dear, some of the boys have started a second men's day at the club and they've asked if I'd like to join them. Think it would look bad if I started playing Tuesdays as well as my normal Thursdays?" A six handicap, Rogers' passion for golf had received considerable criticism from his parishioners.

"I don't mind, honey, but you know how some of your flock feel about your time on the course. Try it for a while and see if anyone complains," his wife, Sue, advised.

Mrs. Brooks worked only part time. She never worked Tuesdays or Thursdays. Reverend Rogers schemed to devote Tuesdays to taking care of Mrs. Brooks; he was already skipping the lunches following Thursday's men's day golf and going directly to her home for afternoon sex.

The following Tuesday morning Rogers left his home quite early and drove directly to Angela's residence. They made love through the morning until both were exhausted and famished. Over breakfast, Angela asked, "So where are you supposed to be this morning, Daniel? What excuse did you tell your wife today?"

"Uh, I just told her I was playing golf."

"And where did you tell her you were playing?"

"Just with some guys at the club," Daniel said.

"Uh, huh. You do know that Tuesdays are Ladies Days, right? Men can't tee off until after 1:00 pm. Hope Sue's not up on your club rules," Angela said.

Oh, shit! How could I have forgotten that? What if Sue realizes I lied? "Uh, she probably wouldn't think of that. She's not a golfer."

"I know that, but I used to see her meet some of the ladies from church at the club for lunch after they finished their rounds. You know, she's going to find out about us sooner or later," Angela said.

"Why would you say that? We've been careful! She doesn't have to find out!"

"Darling, we've been seeing each other for nearly two years now. Don't you think she's at least a little bit suspicious? I sure would be! And I'm tired of being careful!"

Reverend Daniel Rogers felt the blood drain from his face. *Oh, my God!*

Too obvious to be real? Ridiculous for a reasonably intelligent, relatively sophisticated preacher to expect to carry on an affair indefinitely, without getting caught? Especially a man so visible within the community?

Men becoming careless about their affairs is a story I heard often. It seems the longer an indiscretion continues, and the more lies the man tells to cover his tracks, the less he believes that he will ever be exposed.

Flash: "What do you mean you're tired of being careful?' What did you expect to happen? I've never said I'd leave Sue!"

"You sure led me to believe you would! You said our sex was the best you could ever imagine! You said you couldn't get through your days if you didn't have me to rely on! Daniel, it's been two years! I want things to change!" Angela said.

Holy Christ!

Flash: "But I never said things would change! I could never give up my church! Or Sue and the boys! I've never lied to you! Be reasonable," the reverend pleaded.

"You did lie! You said you couldn't get through your days without me!' What'd you expect? That this could go on forever? That you just keep coming here and fucking me whenever you wanted?"

At that moment, Reverend Daniel Rogers saw his world slipping away. He instinctively knew it was only a matter of time before Angela revealed their affair.

"Please! Let's just end this and stay friends! Please!"

"Just end it, after two years of my life devoted to taking care of you?

Stay friends? It's all just been free love to you? Get out of my house! Now!" Angela screamed.

Reverend Rogers' car was in Angela's garage. He barely avoided scraping the passenger's door in his haste to depart. He drove straight to the golf club where his wife's Jeep sat right in the front row of the parking lot.

Flash: "Hello, dear! We all forgot we couldn't tee off until after the ladies finished! We're gonna play around 1:30. May I join you ladies for lunch?"

That evening Reverend Rogers explained to Sue,

Flash: "You know, I'm really worried about poor Angela Brooks. I'm afraid she's misinterpreted my sympathy. I'm going to have to put a little distance in that relationship so she doesn't get the wrong idea about my concern for her wellbeing."

Rogers began laying the groundwork for denying any allegations of infidelity that Angela Brooks might bring.

Following services the next Sunday, Reverend Rogers stood shaking hands with his parishioners as was his custom. Angela Brooks leaned in close to Rogers and whispered, "You'd better call me later today!"

"Angela, please, can't we just end this thing before everybody gets hurt?" Rogers pleaded from his cell phone Sunday evening.

"I'm already hurt! Can't you just tell Sue that you love me! You can make her understand!"

Flash: "Angela, Sue's pregnant again," Rogers lied. "I can't leave her now."

"I thought you said you weren't sleeping with her! Is there anything you told me the truth about?"

In fact, Reverend Rogers had lied to Angela about virtually everything. One month later, an anonymous letter was sent directly to every household in Rogers' congregation describing in detail his affair with Angela Brooks.

Reverend Daniel Rogers lost his church and Sue divorced him. Rogers never admitted the affair to anyone.

Eight years later, remarried and re-established as the pastor of a much smaller church in rural Texas, Reverend Rogers initiated a sexual liaison with a twenty year old girl in the choir. It lasted nearly two years and ended just as tragically as his first infidelity.

Describing the circumstances of his second divorce to me after a round of golf, Rogers swore that the two affairs were the only two *bad things* he ever did. When asked if he felt he could avoid such behavior in the future Rogers said, "Only if I never meet another woman as appealing as Angela or Ashley (the choir girl). I just couldn't help myself."

"I just couldn't help myself" was repeated to me by more than half the men describing their *First Flash Reaction* to certain women. As in Reverend Rogers' case, a first devastating personal experience seems not to prevent reoccurrences, so powerful are some *First Flash Reactions*.

PHASE V

AGES 36-55

PERFECTING THE BALANCING

OF LYING AND LIFE

RONALD BUSH, 39, THE BUDDY LIE SYNDROME

Though not as traumatic as turning fifty, birthday number forty causes many men to begin their first serious self reflection. Forty just sounds a lot older than thirty-nine. *Older* women are now over forty! The large percentage of confidants that told *turning forty* stories often described situations whereby buddies got them in trouble by involving them in their own lying extravaganzas.

Ronald Bush began to mysteriously dread his fortieth birthday the day he turned thirty-nine.

"Remember Dear, next year you'll be in another decade!" Ron's wife, Alice, told him at his thirty-ninth birthday party. "Hope you don't begin any midlife crises!"

Midlife crises my ass! I'm holding up way better than you are!

Flash: "Thanks a lot, honey! I'm always happy to be reminded I'm five years older than you," Ron said.

"Hey, Ron! Maybe next year I'll buy you a cane, buddy!" Ron's friend Eddie said.

"You bring me a cane and I'll wrap it around your little pointed head!"

Eddie and Ron had been best friends since high school. They insulted one another constantly, but, in fact, each man relied on the other for the male support all men need. "Hey, buddy, I need to speak to you privately when we can get away from the wives," Eddie whispered.

Later, as their wives were tidying up the kitchen, Eddie and Ron went out to the garage for a smoke. "When we gonna give up these damn cigarettes, buddy? I think they're causing me this frigging cough I can't seem to shake!" Eddie said.

"What would we use for an excuse to get away from the girls so we can talk guy talk?" Ron countered.

"Good point! And I really need some guy advice right now! What are you doing next Saturday?"

"I don't know. Just hanging out, I guess. What's up?" Ron asked.

"Well, I need some cover! Can you go somewhere out of your house and tell Alice you're with me? All day?" Eddie asked.

"What are you into now, asshole? Don't tell me you're seeing Beth again! If Gail catches you she'll cut 'em off!"

"Uh, no, not Beth. That's all done. Got a new possibility! Her name is Cindy. Met her at that seminar last week! Wait'll you see her!" Eddie said.

"I don't want to meet her! You nearly got me killed over Beth! Don't you ever learn? You're gonna get caught again sure as hell! Damn, Ed, you're livin' on the edge!"

"Hey, it's just gonna be this one time! Cindy said her live-in guy's out of town and for me to come on over and get acquainted. Can't pass up an invitation like that!"

"Did you tell her you're married, dickhead? It'd be way easier if you started with some element of the truth this time!" Ron told his friend.

"Of course not! What do think I am, crazy? I told her I'm in the process of a divorce! That way I have an excuse for limited availability! Will you do it? Please?"

"God damn it, Eddie! Okay, but just this once! I'm not gonna let you screw up my marriage too!"

Later that evening when Eddie and Gail had gone home, Ron told Alice,

Flash: "Hey, honey, Ed and I are going to a car auction up in Columbus next Saturday. Probably be gone most of the day. He's still looking for a '60 Chevy, and there's supposed to be several of them there."

"Okay, but you'll be home for dinner won't you? Remember, my folks are coming over."

Flash: Oh, shit! I forgot! "Sure, we won't be that late."

The following Saturday Ron dutifully left home at 8:00 am to provide his buddy, Ed, with the full-day excuse he requested. With all day to kill, Ron actually drove to Columbus by himself and walked around the car auction for several hours. Just as he was about to leave, someone tapped him on the shoulder. "Hey, son-in-law! I thought we might see you here! You remember my pal Jimmy! Tried to catch you before you left this morning so the four of us could ride together. Great assortment of cars, huh? Where's Ed?"

Son of a bitch! Now what do I do?

Flash: "Uh, Ed found a Chevy he's really interested in. The owner is gonna let him drive it back home to see how it handles. They just left. The guy lives real close to Eddie." Now my Goddamn buddy is causing me to lie to my father-in-law so Alice doesn't get suspicious and talk to Gail! Son of a bitch!

"Eddie got the cash to buy a hobby car? I thought they were trying to have another kid," Ron's father-in-law asked. "Hey, I might as well ride back with you. We're coming to your house for dinner you know."

"Sure. That'll be fine."

On the drive back home Ron's father-in-law asked, "Was it that turquoise blue '60 convertible that Eddie's testing? The one that had the factory four-speed? Me and Jimmy were actually looking at that one just before we ran into you."

Flash: "Uh, no. It was a red hardtop." Where does this end? How many fibs am I gonna have to tell to cover for Ed? This is insane!

"Didn't see a red hardtop. Automatic or standard?"

Flash: "Uh, I think it was a powerglide. We looked at so many I'm not sure."

At the dinner table that evening, Pop started on the car auction again. "Me and Jimmy finally found Ronnie around 3:00 pm. Eddie was already gone. He's buying a '60 hardtop, right? The owner was letting him test it on the way home."

"I thought Eddie was going to drive his car to Columbus, dear! Why do you always have to drive every time you guys go somewhere?" Alice asked.

Flash: "Uh, I just decided at the last minute to take my car. Guess it turned out to be a good decision so Ed could test his '60."

"Oh! So he already bought it? I'm gonna call Gail right now and see if she likes it." Alice exclaimed.

Shit! Shit! Shit!

Flash: "Uh, no! Eddie didn't buy it as far as I know. Better wait to call Gail. I'm not sure she's all that clued in to Eddie's car plans." Ron could feel himself starting to sweat.

Alice shot Ron a look that said she smelled a rat. *God damn Ed! Now what?*

When her parents finally went home, Alice was waiting. "Ronald! What's going on? I'm not buying that '60 Chevy story for one minute! It's a good thing my father ran into you, or I'd think you and that asshole friend of yours were both up to something!"

Flash: "Come on, Alice! You can't get mad at me because my friend is car shopping! Give me a break!"

"Was Ed even with you today? I smell big trouble, mister! You're lucky as hell my dad can vouch for you! You better stay away from Ed! He's pure trouble! Always has been! I'm going to bed!"

Monday morning Ron called Ed at his office. "God damn you, dickhead! You nearly got me killed!" Ron then related the events of the previous Saturday to his friend. "Don't ever ask me to cover for you again!"

"You don't think Alice will tell Gail about her suspicions, do you?" Ed asked.

"Who knows?"

"Hey, buddy, Cindy's got a friend named Sandy you just gotta meet!

Tits just as big as hers!"

Stories of men covering for their buddies' affairs could fill a second book. Phase IV men told me endless tales of how helping other guys deceive their wives and girlfriends almost came back to haunt them. Nevertheless, the men continued to help their buddies lie. It's a guy thing.

"You never know when you're going to need your buddy's help," most men summarized.

Second-hand lying is a classic subset of Borderline Lying. There is always an element of truth around maniacally complicated situations that require real creativity to *pull it off.*

BACHELORS LIE BEST

A large percentage of the men who confided in me were married, but some *confirmed bachelors* also shared stories about their female relationships. The bachelors fell into two distinct sub-groupings:

- Bachelors who lied to women about absolutely everything (the majority)

- Bachelors who lied to women about nearly everything (the minority)

MAJORITY OF
CONFIRMED BACHELORS

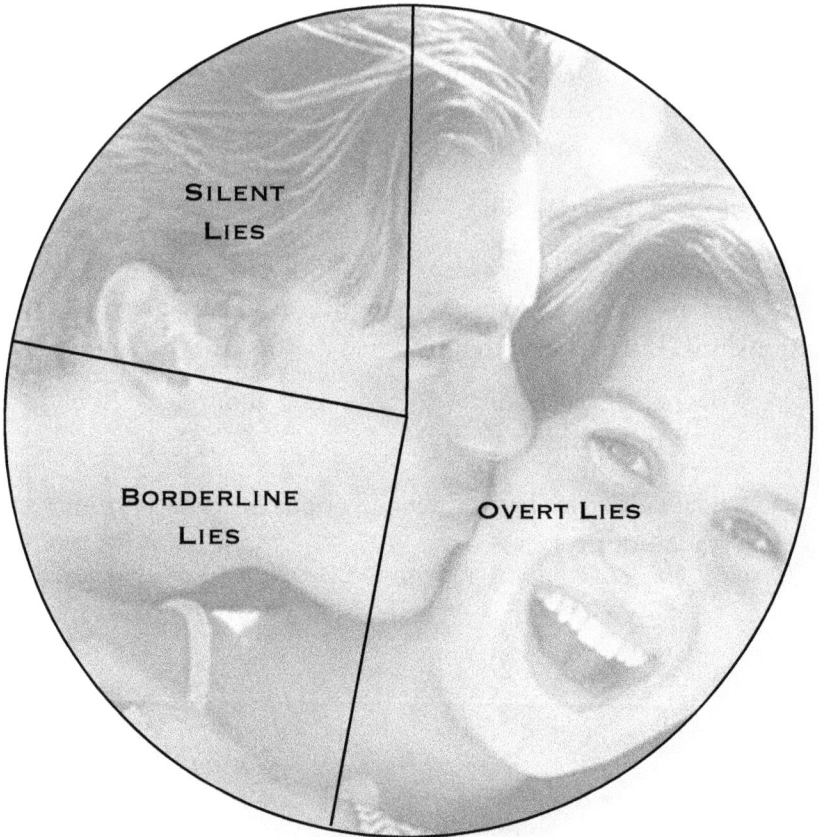

SILENT
LIES

BORDERLINE
LIES

OVERT LIES

BACHELORS WHO LIED TO WOMEN
ABOUT NEARLY EVERYTHING (THE MAJORITY)

MINORITY OF
CONFIRMED BACHELORS

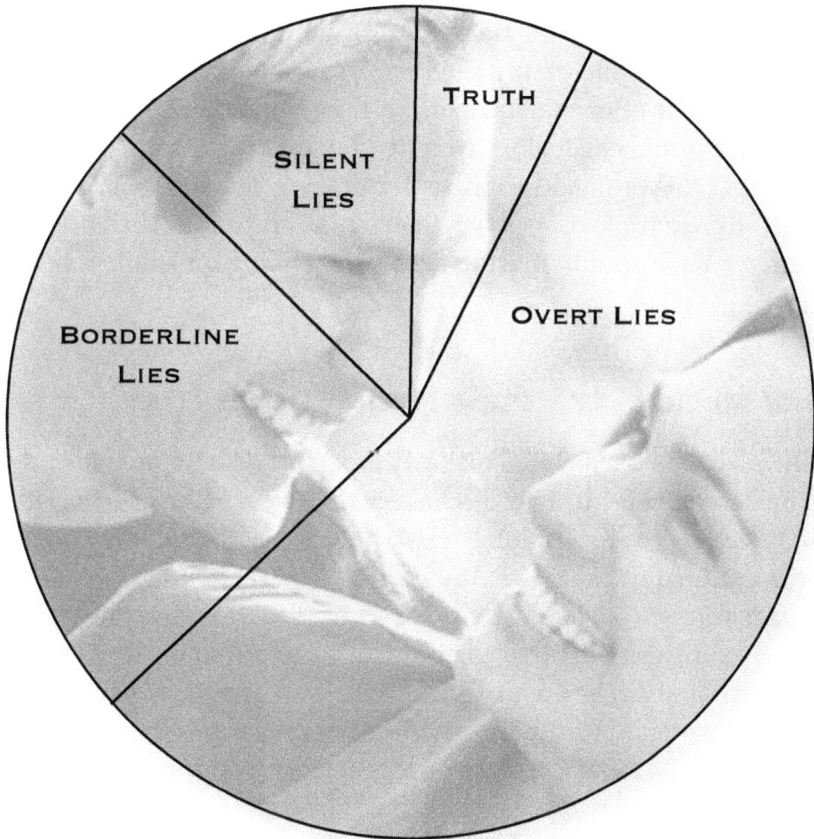

TRUTH

SILENT
LIES

OVERT LIES

BORDERLINE
LIES

BACHELORS WHO LIED TO WOMEN
ABOUT NEARLY EVERYTHING (THE MINORITY)

The majority of bachelors were men who experienced extreme *First Flash Reactions* to women and wanted to spread their sexual escapades over as many women as possible. These men had abandoned any pretense of ever even attempting to be truthful where females were concerned. There were no limits to what they would say or do to get women to sleep with them. Generally, majority group bachelors moved on from woman to woman quite quickly, seldom dating any woman longer than a few months. Younger men in this group often described having multiple affairs going on concurrently; older guys usually stated that it was just easier to pursue one woman at a time, but switch more frequently.

Minority group bachelors weren't that different from the majority except that they tended to stay with the same woman a bit longer. This seemed to require interspersing elements of truth into their *First Flash Reaction* pursuit routines just to keep things going for a longer period of time.

MIKE MCCOY, 42, BEEN THERE, DONE THAT

Mike McCoy is a devoted majority group bachelor who'd worked with me on several consulting projects over the years. Mike's stories of *First Flash Reactions* were absolutely classic; he is the only man who has two stories featured in *Why Men Must Lie*.

At age forty-two Mike had his life set up exactly the way he wanted it. Mike lived in a small, but elegant ocean-view condo in the Marina Del Mar community near Los Angeles. Mike liked to surf, drive his Porsche, and chase women. A former Navy Seal, he was a world-renowned expert on small arms, military explosives, and defensive perimeter construction techniques applied to civilian situations. His consulting assignments took him all over the world and he loved life on the road. Mike kept himself in excellent physical condition and always had a perfect *California tan*. Women found him extremely attractive.

Sitting at breakfast one morning in Paris with a group of men that had just completed a four-month consulting project with the French government, one of Mike's associates asked, "How'd you do with that

German gal last night who kept teasing you at dinner?"

"You know, I was pretty tired, so I just went to bed," Mike said.

"You gotta be kidding! She was stunningly beautiful! You gettin' old McCoy?"

"Nope. Been there, done that," Mike said.

"What do you mean, 'been there, done that?'"

"Just what it sounds it like. That lady was friendly because I knew her from a couple of weeks ago. Remember the only two-day break we took on this project? I spent those two days with her, so been there, done that.' Besides I can't remember everything I told her," Mike said.

"Like what?" another one of McCoy's associates asked. "If I'd been with a woman that beautiful, I'd remember everything!"

"Well, for starters, I can't remember what I told her my name was! I never tell women my real name cause I don't want 'em bugging me. I forget what name I used with her, that's all." McCoy said it so matter-of-factly that all the men were surprised.

"Christ, Mike! You have a reputation as an honorable, completely reliable, highly trusted security consultant! But you don't even tell women your real name? Why?"

"Because I'm not gonna be with 'em long enough for it to matter! A few girls back home know my real name, but not many. Every time I have a mental lapse and tell a woman the truth, it always comes back to bite me. I'm definitely not interested in a long term relationship, so might as well set it up on the front side to make it easy to leave. As in, if they can't find you, they can't bug you!' Now do you get it?"

I just couldn't resist asking McCoy another question. "So, lying to all these women who seem to find you so irresistible doesn't bother you?"

Mike turned the question around. "I'll answer that question in a minute, but first let me ask you something. Do you always tell women the truth about everything?"

"Uh, no."

"Was there ever any woman in your entire life that you told the truth to all the time? Never lied to her once about any little thing?"

"Uh, no."

"Do you withdraw your question to me?" Mike asked. "Actually, I want to answer your question. No, it never bothers me one bit lying to women. The difference between me and all you guys is that I'm 100% honest with you about my attitude toward women! I know what I want from women and I know what I don't want! I want good sex with no complications. That absolutely requires lying to women 100% of the time!"

Mike McCoy's confirmed bachelor attitude toward women was typical of all the bachelors who confided in me. Mike will be the subject of a follow-up story in Phase VII.

Walt Garr, 45, A Truly Hurtful Lie

"Won't Christmas with my parents be fantastic? We haven't seen snow since we've been married! And my sisters will be there with their kids! I'm so excited!" Linda Garr was hugging her husband so tightly he could barely breathe.

Walt Garr wanted to scream. Eight days in Evergreen, Colorado, with his young wife's parents was as close to torture as anything he could imagine.

"Maybe, you know, we'll get pregnant while we're there!" Linda said.

At forty-five with two grown children from his first marriage, Walt knew keeping Linda happy without children would be extremely difficult, but she was so damn beautiful he determined to give it a try. The seventeen year age difference that seemed so manageable in the beginning of their relationship was causing Walt more problems than he could've thought possible.

When Walt had first met Linda, he'd started lying to her with his first sentence. He'd told her he was single, thirty-nine, and wanted kids. In fact, he was forty-four, almost divorced, and seldom saw his two daughters, ages twenty and twenty-two. The only truth Walt told Linda the night they met was what he did for a living.

"It's so great we can fly free anywhere we want to go! It's the best thing about your job! And I'll be able to take our babies back to see my folks whenever I want!" Linda said.

There it was again, that never-ending reference to kids and pregnancy!

Walt Garr graduated from the Air Force Academy and was still a major in the reserves, flying refueling tankers on weekends. He hoped to reach thirty years in the air force so long as he could keep balancing his reserve career with his day job, flying for Delta Airlines.

Walt's *First Flash Reaction* had caused him a great deal of trouble ever since leaving the academy, but he'd avoided real disaster until he'd seen Linda enter his aircraft some two years past. After ten years of marriage and two kids with his first wife, Walt was determined to stay single and enjoy the perks of being a relatively handsome, divorced Delta pilot, until he met Linda. She was beautiful, young, and came from a very wealthy family. Walt and Linda had moved in together two weeks after they met.

Now, after just one year of marriage, all Linda talked about was having children and moving back to Colorado to be near her family. Linda's parents were only a couple of years older than Walt. Linda's two younger sisters each had children of their own and Linda was feeling sibling pressure to give her folks more grandchildren.

"Honey, you can live anywhere! You're a senior captain, now. Let's move to Denver and that can be your hub," Linda said as they boarded their flight from Atlanta. They'd been upgraded to first class and Walt asked the stewardess for a triple Crown Royal as soon as the plane was airborne.

"Now, don't drink too much, honey. We've got to drive across the mountain to Evergreen when we get there," Linda said. "We're in the big bedroom over the garages with that beautiful fieldstone fireplace. We can build a fire every night and make love. And get pregnant!"

Walt badly needed that Crown Royal. He was trying to work up the courage to tell Linda the doctor had just informed him that his vasectomy was not reversible.

I heard Walt Garr's story some fifteen years after the incident related above actually happened. Recently retired from Delta, Walt was sitting in a golf club bar talking with a dozen or so members, one of whom asked, "Christ, Walt! You didn't tell her you were fixed? Why are you telling us this now?"

"Linda was my second wife; I've had three more since then! I just wondered if any of you guys have as much trouble telling women the truth as I do!"

After a few moments of silence, one of the members said, "Yeah, I'm on wife number three and she's catching on to me right now! It seems the older I get the more I just can't stay away from the next sexy gal I meet!"

Although most men find it easier to talk about their *First Flash Reactions* and the corresponding difficulties one-on-one or in groups of two or three, larger group discussions are not uncommon. After Walt Garr opened up, several other golfers related their indiscretions over the next two hours.

A natural reaction to an admission like Walt Garr's would be to question why any man would enter a relationship, much less a marriage, hiding something as important as the inability to father children. Some men's *First Flash Reaction* is so extreme all concept of reality leaves them in pursuit of a new female conquest.

FAMOUS FIFTIES FOLLIES

So many confidants described their *turning fifty follies* to me that a separate book could be filled with their stories, but a few of the best known public figure examples of *turning fifty First Flash Reactions* are too obvious to omit. Following is a short list of recent scandals, all started when a fifty-ish man's *First Flash Reaction* caused him to lie to his wife, and then escalated into a much larger problem.

David Letterman announced on his live broadcast during 2009 that he had slept with women on his show's staff. He further disclosed that an attempt to blackmail him was the reason he'd decided to go public with admission of affairs when he did. Letterman had been lying to his wife about his *First Flash Reactions* for years.

In 2008, Eliot Spitzer, multi-millionaire Governor of New York and potential candidate for United States President, admitted to paying prostitutes tens of thousands of dollars for sex. After being caught up in an FBI investigation targeting other crimes, phone calls Spitzer made to solicit sexual services linked him directly to lies that cost him his political career. A former state prosecutor, Spitzer had to have known there was a high probability that his womanizing would eventually be exposed. He was forty-nine when his *First Flash Reaction* to women caused him to fall from grace, and revealed that he'd been lying to his wife for years.

Senator John Ensign of Nevada, age fifty, heir to a Las Vegas gambling empire, revealed that his parents had paid his mistress nearly $100,000 to "help her and her family." Ensign's wife said she simply couldn't believe it.

Former Senator from South Carolina and 2004 Vice Presidential Candidate, John Edwards, confessed to a multi-year affair with a former aide that started back when he was *turning fifty*. Edwards' indiscretion that started, of course, with lying to his cancer-stricken wife, has taken him out of contention for future national office.

Governor Mark Sanford of South Carolina continued to lie to his wife about his *First Flash Reaction* to a woman from Argentina until his government funded airline travel to pursue her was exposed, forcing him to confess. Sanford was just shy of his fiftieth birthday when his scandal broke. Sanford's wife, Jenny, released her first book, *Staying True*, in February 2010 in which she describes her side of the governor's affair. Interestingly, although she has divorced her husband of twenty years, she describes him as a *good, caring man*, competent in everything except being truthful with her.

Perhaps the most memorable *First Flash* public lying debacle of all occurred back in 1996 when President Bill Clinton, age fifty, lied to his wife, and the nation, about his *First Flash Reaction* to Monica Lewinsky. His uncontrollable sexual urges got him impeached and nearly cost him the presidency. Clinton just kept on lying about his sexual behavior and has, in fact, never admitted the full details of his relationship with *That woman, Ms. Lewinsky*. Bill Clinton still enjoys incredible popularity and respect throughout the world. He's ranked the second most popular American politician of the 20th century.

How could such visible, intelligent celebrities ever believe they could get away with lying about their *First Flash Reactions?* Did they really think they could keep their sexual behavior secret forever? Are these men simply self destructive to the max?

These six very public examples of *First Flash Reactions* represent the extreme end of the curve. The men knew they were likely to be exposed at some point, but simply couldn't help themselves. Their *First Flash Reactions* caused lying that led to disastrous private and public consequences.

Equally interesting to me were the many *near fifty* men who described the increasing intensity of their *First Flash Reactions* to women, but resisted acting on their desires only because they feared the consequences.

MIKE MILLER, 50ISH, ONE SEMI-HONEST MAN

Mike Miller stood at the center rail of O'Shaunessy's Pub in Dornoch, Scotland, enjoying the admiration of his golfing buddies. A former NFL lineman, Mike had turned his pro-football experience and notoriety into a very successful sports broadcasting career. He was widely recognized around the world and he loved the attention and adoration that came with his fame. Yet another group of O'Shaunessy's patrons had just sent a round of drinks to Mike's group as he regaled them with more sports tales.

I was in O'Shaunessy's with a group of golfing pals and happened to get seated for dinner only a table away from Miller's party later that evening. When the dishes were cleared, after-dinner drinks were ordered and the two tables of Americans introduced themselves and began exchanging stories. After Miller had entertained his new friends with several more sports yarns he was asked the following.

"Hey Mike, great story! You're on the road all the time and you're famous. You must get lots of opportunities with the ladies. How about sharing some of those stories with us?"

"I'll tell you what guys, I do get plenty of offers from the ladies, but I just don't fool around. Don't get me wrong. I'm tempted just about every week, but I've never cheated on my wife!" Miller said.

"Man, if I had your opportunities I'd be in trouble all the time!" another man said. "How do you resist? Why do you resist?"

There were twelve men at two large tables, Miller's group of eight and my foursome. All were between forty-eight and sixty-two years of age and were united only by being Americans in a Scottish pub, fulfilling the dream of playing a few of the fabled golf courses of Scotland. The last question to Mike Miller brought a temporary hush to the group as they awaited his response.

"You know guys, it's interesting," Mike began. "I got married while I was still in college and we already had two kids when I signed with the Raiders. When I went to my first pro training camp it was the first time I'd been away from Ruth and the kids, and I was, of course, a little apprehensive about making it in pro football. I'll be honest; I was scared of failing! I'd been the strongest, fastest lineman at my college, but I quickly realized I was barely average in the big leagues. "Our first *off day* at camp came after two weeks and the wife and kids were back in Jersey, so I went out with some of the guys just to blow off a little steam. There were about a dozen of us sitting around in a group sort of like ours here tonight, but we weren't old farts, like now! Seriously, I was dead tired, but anxious to be accepted by my teammates, when this drop-dead gorgeous gal came over and said, 'Tonight, big boy, I'm gonna rock your world!'"

That brought a combination of laughter and cheers from his audience, but Miller called for quiet. "I probably would have succumbed to her offer, but the old pro whose position I was understudying put his hand on my shoulder and whispered, 'Mikey, if you go with her, that'll be the most expensive piece of tail you'll ever get. She reads the papers, son. She knows you just got a million dollar signing bonus. If you start down that path, it'll shorten your pro career by five years. Think about it.'

"Frankly, it was the fear of a *shortened career* that deterred me!"

"So you didn't go with her?" someone asked.

"No, I did not. She left with her second choice, a tight end who had gotten a half million dollar bonus."

"How many years did that tight end play pro ball?"

"Six seasons longer than I did!" Miller confirmed to the laughter of his comrades. "I still get offers, and I'm still tempted. But fear of what I could lose keeps me straight."

"Are you just not affected by the ladies anymore, then?"

"Gentlemen, every time I see an attractive gal, I wonder 'what would she be like in bed?' I'll bet you guys have the same reaction!" Mike said.

"Not just the pretty ones! All women!" said one of the golfers.

The twelve men ended their evening with a toast to that last proclamation, confirming their *First Flash Reactions* to women, *all women*, whether acted on, or not.

JOE SYKES, 50, WHEN THE *FIRST FLASH REACTION* REALLY KICKS IN

The premise of *Why Men Must Lie* seems to become more pronounced as men mature. Stories from Phase V, ages thirty-six to fifty-five, reveal that men in this group are more likely to act on their *First Flash Reaction* to women than in any other period.

Just when women expect their maturing husbands or partners to be satisfied balancing careers, hobbies, and family obligations, many men are experiencing what they commonly describe as the *missing the boat* syndrome. Men who have resisted their *First Flash Reactions* prior to this phase find themselves wanting to experiment with additional female sex partners *before it's too late*. Instead of being concerned about having too much to lose pursuing new sexual conquests, men in Phase V repeatedly say they reach a point where nothing but a new sexual conquest really matters.

When asked if they're simply caught up in mid-life crises, most men recoil from that concept, stating specifically that all they really need is a *new* or *different* woman. Many go on to say that no form of substitute or diversion diminishes their desire to experiment sexually *before it's too late*.

Do they discuss this potential life-altering circumstance with their spouses or girlfriends? Essentially, never.

During Phase V, men buy Harley Davidson's, Porsches, and Corvettes, and multiple new sets of golf clubs. They take *guy vacations* to fish or hunt and organize poker nights to get out of the house. Wherever they congregate, whatever the venue, if their wives are absent, the number one topic of discussion is always extracurricular sexual activity. In other words, who's having *sex outside his marriage or relationship, how much* and *with whom*.

Joe Sykes was a former GE *whiz kid*. At age fifty, both of his children had graduated from college and were actually on their own, requiring no more funds from dear old Dad. Joe's wife, Diana, came from considerable family wealth; the Sykes' had never wanted for money. They had just purchased their third family home in Naples, Florida, to compliment the ski lodge in Aspen and their main residence in Fairfield, Connecticut.

Joe had always had an eye for the ladies, but fear of jeopardizing his career had kept him on the straight and narrow. Diana's wrath was of secondary concern, but a deterrent nonetheless.

As a GE Vice President, Joe lived the good life. He was well compensated for his seventy hour work weeks, and he considered himself to still be *in the running* for future advancement.

Sykes received the shock of his life shortly after his fiftieth birthday on his twenty-eight year anniversary with General Electric.

"Morning, Joe. You're looking dapper as always. Good weekend? How was the poker game?" Joe's boss asked.

"Morning to you, Bill. Great! Took a hundred bucks off Rayhall and Tibbits, so poker was perfect. How'd you do?"

"Not as good as you. Joe, I'll get right to the point. The company congratulates you on your fine performance last year. Your cash bonus will be near the maximum, and you'll receive a nice array of options to add to your portfolio. Joe, I have your retirement papers right here. The company is *buying* you an additional two years of seniority, bringing you to a full thirty, and maximum retirement benefits for your grade. We appreciate your many years of dedicated service and wish you much happiness in your retirement life."

Joe Sykes was completely stunned. He'd handed out *golden handshakes* to his employees in the past, but never imagined it could happen to him.

"Well, gee, thanks, Bill. I'm a little surprised. How long have..." Joe stopped in mid-sentence, realizing there was no discussion to be had. Joe knew the system. The decision had been made. He was retired as of this minute; a formal dinner would give him a send off at month's end. It was futile to protest. "Thanks."

Joe made his way back to his office literally in shock. He sat back in his leather chair and let out a sigh. *God damn it! How could they do this to me? I'm at the prime of my productive years! I'm in better shape than when I was forty. God damn it!*

Paula Rice, Joe's personal assistant entered his office and said, "I'm so sorry, Joe. I can see how surprised you are. I'm just so sorry."

"You knew before I did? God damn it, why didn't you warn me?" Joe said.

"Joe, you know how it works around here! They told me to support you as you vacated your office and do whatever I can to make it easier. You know I need this job! What else could I do?"

"So you probably know who's replacing me!"

"Yes, Joe, I do. It's Bill Pace from the international desk. He'll be here in about fifteen minutes to debrief with you. Try to be cordial, it's not his fault. He's actually one of your favorites," Paula said. "You really had no idea? No clues that you were on the *early out* list?"

Joe Sykes' expression answered Paula's question. "Didn't even know guys on my level were being considered. What will I tell Diana?"

"Well, you can start by telling her to 'go to hell!' I don't know why you've put up with that bitch all these years anyway!" Paula said.

Paula's outburst was Joe's second shock of the day. He'd sensed that Paula didn't really like his wife, but he had no idea she felt so negative toward her. "What do mean?" Joe asked.

Paula turned and closed the door to Joe's office. "Joe, Diana's in Naples now, right? Last year she spent more time in Colorado and Florida than Fairfield! You two have been on different planets the entire five years I've worked for you! You need to get with it! You're the lonely one, not her!"

"Paula, I just don't underst..." Joe began.

"Bill Pace will be here any moment! Straighten up! Pretend early retirement was your idea! For God's sake Joe, you're free! You're relatively rich! Be a man! Live!" Paula said.

Pace knocked on the office door. "Good time to talk, Joe? Congratulations on your early out! Wish it was me instead of you. Lucky man!" Bill said. "How about a couple of coffees, Paula, I'm sure Joe doesn't want to spend any more time with me than he has to!"

As Paula exited the office she winked at Joe.

While Joe talked with Bill, several associates stopped by to congratulate him on his early retirement *decision.* Joe had regained enough composure to show a professional demeanor, but all he could really think about was what Paula had said about his relationship with Diana.

At lunch time, Bill Pace said, "Joe, we're having a nice 'thank you' luncheon in the executive dining room. I'm just gonna freshen up and meet you there."

Sykes' pay grade entitled him to a private lavatory right in his office. Joe looked at himself in the mirror, trying to prepare himself for the *thank you* gathering that he absolutely had to attend. *What a system! Twenty-eight years of dedication and out the door in a day. And what the hell did Paula mean about Diana? Why haven't I even tried to call my wife?*

As Joe walked by Paula's desk, she softly said, "I'll buy drinks after work. Don't make any commitments to those guys!"

By mid-afternoon, Joe had talked with Bill Pace for as long as he could endure. At 4:30 Paula brought in boxes and said that she'd be glad to pack Joe's few personal effects in the office and send them to him.

"Have you told Diana yet?" Paula asked.

"Uh, no. She's in Naples until next Monday. Maybe I'll just fly down and tell her," Bill said.

"Is that what you really want to do? Come on, I promised you a drink! Meet me at The Rock over in Trumbell; we can have some privacy there," Paula said.

After his third martini, Joe asked Paula, "What'd you mean 'tell her to go to hell'? Why don't you like Diana?"

"Do you really like her, Joe? Is she who you want to spend the next thirty years with? You've been with GE twenty-eight years. Now that's done. Isn't it time to do something you want to do? I've seen you look at me when you think I'm not watching. I've seen you look at lots of other women in the office. And at Christmas parties. Tell me the truth, Joe. What do you really want, now that GE doesn't own you anymore?"

Joe Sykes made love to Paula all that night, and the next two. He stayed in her condo, going home only to pick up more clothes. Joe thought about his life and what he wanted from the next thirty years. He called Diana every night, but never mentioned his retirement.

"Hi, babe. How's the weather down there? Playing lots of golf? How about tennis? Been to Campiello's?" Joe asked Diana.

Just before Paula came home from work on the fourth day, Joe called his wife in Naples.

Flash: "Diana, you're just not gonna believe what I'm about to say. I was told today that all executives at my level will be offered incredibly lucrative early retirement packages. Even guys as young as me. I may receive my offer as early as tomorrow. What do you think of that?"

After a pause Diana said, "I think you should keep working, dear. You're way too young to retire. What would you do all day?"

"Well, we'll see. Won't hurt to study the package," Joe said.

"By the way, honey, if you don't mind I think I'll stay in Naples another week. Weather's so good and I really have nothing going up there," Diana said.

Paula's right, she is a bitch. "Sure, hon, want me to fly down for the weekend?"

"I've got golf with the girls both days, but come if you want," Diana said.

"I'll call you tomorrow. Good night," Joe said and hung up.

Joe took Paula out to dinner that night in a town several miles away.

Flash: "I'm gonna fly down and tell Diana tomorrow," Joe started.

"Tell her what? That you're already retired, or about us?"

Flash: "Christ! Not anything about us! I'm just going to explain about retirement options," Joe said.

"Why don't you wait 'til Monday? We could spend the weekend together. Maybe go into the city. Diana won't care!" Paula said.

Flash: "Naw, I told her I was coming."

That Thursday was the last night Joe spent with Paula. On Friday he flew to Las Vegas and spent each weekend day with a different prostitute.

Joe didn't tell his wife that he was retired for another month. Joe Sykes' *First Flash Reaction* to women controlled his existence for the next twenty years. Sykes told me that as near as he could figure, he never told any woman the truth about anything again.

Joe Sykes' story of concealing his *First Flash Reaction* to women until he finally felt secure enough to act on his desires was a common pattern described by many confidants. Very often a significant event in a man's life provides the motivation to cause him to respond to his previously repressed *First Flash Reaction* impulses.

TONY DEITZ, 53, STILL LYING TO HIS MOTHER

Anthony "Tony" Dietz walked out of the courthouse and screamed for joy. This was the moment he'd been waiting for more than twenty years. His divorce was final. Tony was a free man.

"So how's it feel, buddy? As good as you'd hoped it would?" Tony's lawyer and good friend, William Bask asked.

"Oh God, yes! We've been at each others' throats for twenty years. Why the hell I didn't do this sooner I just don't know!"

Walking with Bask and Dietz was Tony's best friend, Jimmy Crandall. "I know why, pal! You've been afraid to tell your mother that you've got a girlfriend. Long as you were still married to Joan, you didn't have to fess up about Delia."

"You know, Crandall, I ought to just kick your ass right now! I'm not afraid to tell Ma about Delia. It's just that Ma still likes Joan. Christ, she takes her side on everything. She would probably have testified in Joan's behalf if she knew about Del," Tony said.

"Well, pal, you're gonna have to tell her now!"

For years, Tony had assured his mother that everything was fine between him and his wife. Lately, his mother had been questioning him constantly about how he and Joan were getting along, and Tony just kept lying, saying "everything's fine."

Despite years of frustration with his wife, it was only three months previous that he finally demanded a divorce. Tony had given Joan everything she wanted in the settlement just to get it over with quickly, and in exchange for Joan agreeing not to tell his mother until the divorce was final.

Actually, not really everything Joan might have demanded had she known Tony had been hiding money in Swiss accounts for more than twenty-five years. She had no idea of his true, total net worth. Tony had been lying to Joan about his *outside* income ever since they were married. That's how he'd been able to finance his womanizing, his "secret" apartment, and, in fact, his secret life with a long string of ladies including his latest fling, Delia.

"Are you gonna go tell your mom, now that you actually are divorced?" Crandall asked. "You know, your mom reads the papers! You'd better tell right now, chicken little!"

"Awright! Awright! Christ, you're a worse nag than Joan! I'm going over to tell Ma right now, just get off my back, will ya?" Dietz was about ready to punch his pal.

"Six to one he doesn't tell her about Del," Crandall said to William Bask. "Wanna put a C-Note on it?"

"And how will we know for sure if he does?" asked the lawyer. "I'd have to hear it directly from Mrs. Dietz before I'd believe it!"

"You can both go to hell!" Tony said. "I'm headed to Ma's right now. And I'm gonna tell her everything!"

Tony sat outside his mother's home for nearly a half hour trying to get his courage up. Finally, he went inside. "Hi Ma. How's it going? Here's some of those Godiva chocolates you like so much."

"Hi Honey! What are you doing here in the middle of the day? Aren't you working?"

Flash: "Uh, Ma, I need to talk to you. I just came from the courthouse. Joan divorced me, Ma. After all these years, she just wanted out. What do think?"

Tony's mother stared at her son for a very long time before she spoke. "I just don't believe it! When did this start? Why didn't you and Joan come talk to me? What's wrong with her? I thought it was odd that she hadn't been coming around like she used to! My God! Do the kids know? What do they think? Are they okay? My God! How could she do this?"

Tony was relieved that his mother immediately calculated that the divorce had to be Joan's fault. He'd counted on that.

Flash: "I guess she just wanted out, Ma. Guess I'm not as cute as I was thirty-five years ago. Seriously, I'm just not sure why."

"And she kept it from me? She didn't talk to me about it? I could have helped her! My God! That bitch! Are you going to be okay, dear? What will you do? Is Joan staying in the house? Did you just give her everything? Where will you live? You can always come back here, Honey!" Tony's mom said.

Flash: "Well, Mom, we didn't want to upset you until we were sure we were gonna go through with it. I tried to talk her out of it right up 'til the last minute, but it was what she wanted. So now it's done. I'm sorry, Ma. Are you mad?"

"Just shocked right now, Son. Where will you go? Will you have enough money? Will the kids get through this?"

"Ma, the kids have lives of their own. They'll be fine. Actually, they weren't that surprised, After all, they're both over thirty. I already got a small apartment downtown. I'll be okay after I get used to it. Ma, I gotta go take care of some things. I'll come by later and we can talk."

"Why would Joan do this?"

Flash: "I don't know, Ma. I just don't know."

Tony Dietz never told his mother the truth about his divorce. He never told her about Delia or the ladies who came later. His mother was so upset with his former wife that Joan never got to tell Mrs. Dietz her side of the story.

Men's inability to tell their mother's the truth about divorces was a constant theme I heard over the years. Most men expressed regret that they couldn't confide in their mothers and the few men who did never admitted that their *First Flash Reactions* caused most, if not all of their marital problems.

JAMES CALDWELL, 54, CARS TO KISSES

My business career spanned the last third of the twentieth century; a period during which women began competing with men for promotion and power in their chosen career fields. Whether in education, business, broadcasting or even the military, women in the western world essentially achieved professional parity with their male counterparts like never before. This set up new dynamics in male-female relationships about which much has been written and analyzed as scholars have attempted to explain the challenges this has caused both sexes.

James Caldwell was an admitted *car addict.* He simply loved automobiles and had focused his professional life on climbing the ladder at GM so he could immerse himself into the automotive industry. James graduated from General Motors Institute and earned his masters' degree in engineering from the University of Michigan. His personal collection included a vintage Ferrari and five other classic cars. Caldwell's career path at GM started in plant management and then advanced through corporate engineering, eventually landing him a corner office in world headquarters with global responsibility.

At age fifty-four James was still on the promotable list and aspired to become a group vice president. Having worked the obligatory eighty hour weeks for more than thirty years, James openly joked that his wife had raised their three children as a *single parent*. Caldwell's devotion to his career had kept him on a straight and narrow behavior path at GM; his only distraction being the pursuit of more collectible cars for personal enjoyment.

Throughout his work life, James had reported to equally ambitious and dedicated corporate climbers, all men slightly older than him and similarly consumed by their careers. Even in the early 1990's GM was pretty much an *old boys' organization,* and James was an established member of the club. His current boss, Bill Head, was a group vice president and had been one of James' mentors for years.

"Jim, how goes it? Are we ever going to get to go home for dinner? I can't remember the last time we left here before 9:00 pm. But great work bringing that new V-6 power train on stream. Wouldn't have happened without your leadership! Thanks!" Head said.

"Well, thanks for the compliment, Bill. I truly appreciated it. Maybe we'll catch Camry after all!"

"Wouldn't that be nice. Hey, Jim, you know we've got some outsiders coming in to our organization at the board's insistence. The board wants to consolidate stateside engineering with what Opel does in Europe. We'll have the first senior vice president in GM's history that isn't *homegrown.* Her name is Catherine Pierce-Hall. She'll be taking my spot effective next month. I'm going to take a sweetened *early out* to make way for her. Jim, she'll be your boss. I know you'd hoped to get my slot, and, frankly, I'd hoped you would too. But it's a done deal. You'll meet her at her press announcement on Friday. What do you think?" Head asked.

Though stunned, James said, "Wow. Bit of a surprise. Have you met her, Bill?"

"I have. She's impressive, Jim. And quite a looker. I think she's still in her thirties."

"What? Where does she come from? Does she know anything about cars? Under forty? That's another first for GM far as I can recall." Caldwell was struggling to keep his cool. *A new senior VP from the outside? A woman, no less! Under forty? My boss?*

"She comes from the aircraft industry, Jim. She'll have worldwide responsibility for all new power train development as well as small platform engineering. You'll like her. She's really sharp."

Easy for Bill Head to say! He doesn't have to report to her.

James Caldwell and all of Ms. Pierce-Hall's direct reports were introduced to her at a luncheon following her press announcement. Fourteen General Motors Vice Presidents, all men, awaited Ms. Pierce-Hall in the top floor executive dining room at World Headquarters. The men had worked together for years and there was a degree of camaraderie within the group that usually made for spirited conversations preceding meetings. This day, however, the dining room was eerily silent.

Bill Head held the door for Ms. Pierce-Hall's grand entrance. Although the assembled VP's had seen press photos of their new boss, none were prepared for how incredibly beautiful she was in person.

"Gentlemen," Head began, "May I present Catherine Pierce-Hall." As Head elaborated on her education and experience, James Caldwell sat transfixed. His new senior vice president was the most beautiful woman he'd ever seen, exactly the features he admired, and a smile to melt gold.

Ms. Pierce-Hall went around the table, shaking hands with her direct reports. Her grip was strong and firm; she held Caldwell's hand just a moment longer than necessary. "James, I am so pleased to meet you! I've read your papers on electro-mechanical power train development, and I agree completely with your vision for battery power-to-wheel development. I'm sure we are going to build the best electric cars in the world…together."

James Caldwell could manage only a muted "thank you." *Why does she have to be so damn gorgeous? Her voice is magnificent! She exudes power…physical power. Damn!*

Pierce-Hall spoke for twenty minutes, expressing her pleasure at having been selected to her new position. She said all the right stuff. The VPs were impressed.

"And Jim, if your schedule allows, I'd really appreciate meeting with you right after lunch. I want to understand where we're at with the Opel technology right away. I'm traveling to Germany over the weekend to be introduced at Opel's executive engineering staff meeting Monday," Pierce-Hall said.

Following the luncheon Caldwell and Pierce-Hall met in his office to discuss battery power-to-wheel engineering coordination with GM's Opel Division. Pierce-Hall actually took notes. Their discussion lasted two hours.

"Jim, get your girl to bring us some coffee. I need to hit the head," Catherine said. "Then I've got just a couple more questions and I'll let you go. And please start calling me Caty. All my close friends do."

My girl? Caty? Hit the head? What's this woman up to?

"Cream or sugar?" James asked.

"Straight black, sweetie!" Ms. Pierce-Hall said.

"Sweetie?" Holy shit! This woman is dangerous!

When Pierce-Hall returned from the *head*, Caldwell introduced her to *his girl*, Mrs. Betty Rush, who had been a GM executive secretary for thirty years.

"Nice to meet you, Mrs. Rush. Leave us. Jim and I have lots more to talk about," the new group vice president said.

"Jim, while I was peeing I decided I need you to come to Opel with me tomorrow. We can fully debrief on the flight, and I'll be totally up to speed to deal with my German staff. I need to hit the ground running to straighten out this mess, and I've decided you're my 'go-to' guy stateside. Wheels up at 7:00 am so we can get rested and ready Sunday. Okay?" Ms. Pierce-Hall said.

"Okay. Sure. Other staff going?"

"Just you and me, sweetie! We'll knock 'em dead! Oh, bring casuals in case we feel like sight-seeing Sunday afternoon! See you in the am. *Ciao!*"

James Caldwell sat staring at the door through which Pierce-Hall had departed. He could not remember feeling as confused as he was at that moment. *Where in the hell did she come from? What's she trying to do? What's with the language? You and me, sweetie? We'll knock 'em dead? Why does she have to be perfect?*

Caldwell called Mrs. Rush to his office. "Betty, Ms. Pierce-Hall just informed me that I'm to accompany her to Germany tomorrow. You'll have to reschedule everything on my calendar next week. Please have a driver pick me up at home at 5:00 am. Guess we're on Pierce-Hall time, now."

"Yes sir. Other staff going?" Mrs. Rush asked.

Flash: "Uh, I'm not sure. Guess I'll find out in the morning, Betty. Thanks, and have a good weekend. See you in a week!"

Caldwell then called his wife.

Flash: "Hey, honey. I've just been added to the staff accompanying our new boss to Opel tomorrow. You'll have to cancel our weekend plans. And could you please look at my business casual clothes? Guess we're going to 'dress down' a bit for plant tours under the new regime. Looks like I'll be in Europe all week, so next weekend may be catch-up time here. Sorry, you know what happens under a new group VP. See you in an hour or two; I've got some organizing to do here."

James Caldwell sat staring at the phone over which he'd just told his wife the first lies he could remember. And Mrs. Rush would undoubtedly check the flight manifest and see that he'd lied to her about "other staff" going to Germany. These would be the first of hundreds of lies that James Caldwell would tell his wife and his secretary over the coming months. His *First Flash Reaction* to Catherine Pierce-Hall had already changed his life.

That weekend James Caldwell and Catherine Pierce-Hall began an affair that lasted three years and became the worst kept secret within General Motors. Their affair culminated with Caldwell's retirement and Pierce-Hall's resignation from GM.

As Caldwell related his story to me and two of his fellow GM VP's, Bill and Fred, one of them asked, "Jim, you knew it couldn't be kept secret for long! Why'd you do it?"

"Guys, I've asked myself that question 10,000 times over the past four years. But sitting here with the three of you, I'll confess. I could no more say *no* to Caty than I could stop breathing. She came into my life at a time when I felt my life was half over, and I was so bored I could've died! I'd always done what people expected of me; not what I wanted to do. My wife was no longer paying any attention to me. I felt there had to be more to life than just my career. But, in truth, I just had to have that woman!"

Caldwell's confession caused both Bill and Fred to squirm in their chairs.

"So, gentlemen, I just couldn't help myself. I'd wanted other women all my life. Caty's timing was right. You guys have never been tempted? Am I the only dirty old man here?" Caldwell asked.

"No, Jim. You're the one of the three of us who got caught," Fred said, "and is willing to talk about it."

RALPH PERKINS, 55, MIDLIFE CRISIS

Nearly every man over forty who confided in me expressed real trepidation about turning fifty. For some, fifty-five is even more difficult. Versions of the following statements were repeated to me again and again:

"My life is half over."

"I've always done what people expected of me; not what I wanted to do."

"I'm so bored I could die."

"There has to be more to life than this."

"My wife no longer pays any attention to me."

When asked what it is they really need to cure their *turning fifty blues* most men admit to unfulfilled sexual desires. Further questioning often exposes years of increasing *First Flash Reactions* to women that men resisted, fearing the consequences of doing what they really wanted to do.

Ralph Perkins dreaded his fifty-fifth birthday more than anything he could remember since receiving his draft notice to report for army basic training. When Ralph graduated from high school in 1964, military service was essentially a foregone conclusion for eighteen year old males who had no form of deferment or physical limitation. Still, he hoped that somehow he could just keep working the graveyard shift at a Ford Motor

Company plant in Dearborn, Michigan. Ralph had worked there for exactly twelve months when the dreaded notice arrived.

Perkins had been dating his high school sweetheart for three years, but still hadn't talked Helen Rinowski into sleeping with him. Sex with Helen was all that Ralph thought about, other than fixing up his '55 Chevy. Ralph recalled that his mind was 95% on Helen and 5% on his Chevy, but 100% of his frustration came from Miss. Rinowski.

"Helen, I got my draft notice today! I've gotta report to Fort Knox in five weeks. Probably be in Vietnam in six months! Now will you sleep with me?" Ralph pleaded.

"Good Catholic girls don't do that, Ralph! You know that! Let's get married right now! Then everything will be perfect," Helen said.

Oh, Shit! She's just not gonna give in! I can't go to war a virgin!

"Okay, Helen, you win! Let's do it!"

"Oh, Ralphy! I love you!"

The marriage license and paper work took three weeks. Ralph and Helen were married in a simple, sweet ceremony in St. Marks Church attended by both families and a few close friends. After a brief honeymoon, Ralph left for Fort Knox.

Three months into a tour in Vietnam and nine months after Ralph got drafted, Helen informed Ralph that he was the father of a baby girl, Rachael Sue Perkins, named after his mother. Helen's parents bought her and the baby an airline ticket to meet Ralph in Hawaii on his R & R from the combat zone, and Helen returned home pregnant again. By the time Ralph was discharged from the army he had two children, ages two years and thirteen months. Ralph was a month shy of his twenty-first birthday when he went back to work at Ford. Now, at age fifty-five, Ralph and Helen had seven children, fourteen grandchildren, a paid-off home in the Detroit suburbs, and a lake cottage in Petoskey, Michigan.

Perkins had thirty-seven years seniority as a United Auto Workers Union electrician, all at the same Ford plant where he'd started before the army. Ford offered all of its union employees a lucrative early retirement incentive that made continuing to work unrewarding. Ralph took the retirement offer and faced the first real *downtime* in his life. Union electricians had been able to work as many overtime hours as they could stand; Ralph had averaged more than eighty hours per week for the last twenty years.

Comfortably secure financially, Ralph had only two problems. He had absolutely nothing to do with his time, and he had never had sex with any woman other than his wife.

I met Ralph at a VFW hall outside Detroit, where I'd joined some former army buddies for a reunion. Ralph was friends with one of the guys, and he joined the group of relative strangers, sharing only the common bond of having served in Vietnam. Several beers into the evening's discussion Ralph shared his life's story with his new group of friends.

"So, Ralph, what's next? You've gotta develop some hobbies or get a part-time job, man! Otherwise you're headed for trouble," a new friend advised.

Ralph reached into his back pocket and produced several sheets of paper, each one a personal profile of a woman interested in *male companionship.*

"I've got it narrowed down to these for starters," Ralph said. "Which one would you guys start with?"

"You're kidding, right, Ralph?" his buddy who'd introduced him to the group said. "Helen will cut your nuts off if she caught you with another woman!"

"Don't care," Ralph said. "I've spent thirty-seven years in that damn plant working my ass off. I've thought about strange pussy every hour of every day I worked. Nothing can stop me from getting some now."

"You're serious!"

"You bet your ass I am! I've done everything I was supposed to do as a father and a grandfather. I've taken care of my wife and she's happy taking care of the grandkids. That's not for me. I'm starting with one of these (women from the lists) and I'm gonna keep going 'til I'm satisfied!"

"Why'd you wait until now?"

"Really don't know, but I'm not waiting any longer!" Ralph said.

At the end of the evening the new *buddies* all agreed to stay in touch, exchanging phone numbers and email addresses. Of course, none of them actually made the effort to get together again.

Six years later, I was attending an army reunion at Fort Bragg, North Carolina, when Ralph tugged on my sleeve. "Remember me? Ralph Perkins from Detroit? Met you at the VFW hall the night you were visiting Frank Couch a few years back."

"How could anyone forget you, Ralph? You were about to 'break out' as I recall. Did you ever really do it?"

Perkins once again reached into his pocket, and brought out a photo collection of some twenty women. On the back of each picture were two dates, usually two to three months apart.

"Here's my scorecard," Ralph said. "Let me buy you a beer and I'll tell you about each one."

Preposterous coincidence? No man would talk so openly to strangers? Maintaining picture *evidence* too foolish to believe? The story is accurate in every detail. Over the next two hours Ralph recounted each conquest.

"Still married to Helen? What does she think you're doing when you're chasing skirts?"

"I have fishing rods and golf clubs. She probably suspects, but never asks. Busy with the grandkids, I guess," Ralph concluded.

"Any guilt, Ralph?"

"About what?" Ralph responded.

Ralph's mounting frustration with not acting on his *First Flash Reactions* was another often-repeated story I heard, particularly from recently retired men in their fifties. When men wait so long to exercise their *First Flash Reactions* they often do it to the extreme.

PHILIP B. STORM

ANALYSIS OF PHASES I-V, UP TO AGE 56

So far, *Why Men Must Lie* has focused on men fifty-five years and younger. Does the inability to be truthful with the women in their lives mitigate as men age? Does a diminished sex drive make it easier for men to communicate what they really want and are thinking as they get older? Do men ever really change at all?

No, no, and no. In fact, men are as uncomfortable communicating with women at age seventy-five as Junior, Billy or Bobby were when they were twelve years old. In fact, being truthful with the women in their lives seems to get markedly more difficult for men as they age, particularly if the issue involves sex. The more sexual the subject is, the more difficulty men have being candid with the women in their lives.

The relatively innocent fibs young boys get used to telling their mothers, female teachers, and first girlfriends form a foundation for lying to women for the rest of their lives. Most interestingly, men fifty-five and younger view lying about their true sexual reactions to women almost like a game. These same men consider themselves to be honest and truthful about their careers and professional interactions with other men. Why do they so consistently lie to women?

The more I listened to the men who confided in me, the more convinced I became that the *First Flash Reaction* truly is the base cause of the lying to women phenomenon. Men in Phases I-V describe their inability to have a first response to women that isn't purely sexually based.

This *First Flash Reaction* usually passes quickly to a secondary response that is more acceptable and expected by modern society, but still, the very first, most relationship-influencing reaction is purely sexual.

James Caldwell knew unequivocally that he had a new female boss on whom he would be dependent for a successful and satisfying conclusion to his thirty-three year General Motors career. Yet he couldn't help but surrender to his *First Flash Reaction* to her. James recalled, "I knew it was absolutely stupid to see her as anything but my new group vice president. But when I saw her in person, all logic and common sense went out the window. I was immediately willing to take any risk, or tell any lie to anybody, to be with her."

Joe Sykes succumbed to his *First Flash Reaction* to multiple women after being freed from career concerns following a forced early retirement. Joe stated, "Once I gave in to my *First Flash Reaction* and had sex with Paula, I was a slave to my pent-up sexual appetite for the rest of my life."

Dr. Lee Fair couldn't bring himself to tell his mother the truth about purchasing a Honda. Forty years later, he was still lying to his mother about the motorcycles he owned.

Charlie Jones gave in to a stripper on the night before his wedding. Charlie said, "Worst thing was, that fast, rough sex with the dancer made me realize what was missing in my sexual relationship with my new wife. I was out chasing two months after I got married!"

Understand these are not isolated, *unusual* incidents. From a sample size of nearly seven hundred men, every one of them described or admitted to *First Flash Reactions* that they simply could not prevent, even if they wanted to.

Remember, too, that the *First Flash Reaction* is often a negative response, but no less the first response. A negative *First Flash Reaction* to a woman in no way increases the man's likelihood of being truthful with her. She's still a female, and the man is equally conditioned to lie to her, even if he has no desire to have sex with her.

PHASE VI

AGES 56-70
ADJUSTING LYING
TO THE NEW REALITIES

VIAGRA ALTERS THE LYING PROBABILITY CURVE

Ever since Pfizer Pharmaceutical Company introduced its erectile dysfunction correction product, Viagra, back in 1998, men in Phases VI and VII have experienced dramatically higher rates of late onset *First Flash Reactions* to women. Perhaps it would be more accurate to say that Phase VI and VII men now have the ability to *work out* or *implement* their *First Flash Reactions* more than ever before.

Older confidants long described *First Flash Reactions* that nearly equaled those of their younger years. Many were, however, deterred from action by the potential embarrassment of not being able to perform sexually prior to the advent of Viagra and competitive drugs such as Cialis and Levitra. There seems to be a direct correlation between Phase

VI and VII men's lying to women and their ability to perform sexually as revealed by the following two graphs. The first example is an early version of the graph that was constructed by me during early 1996:

PROBABILITY CURVE 1996

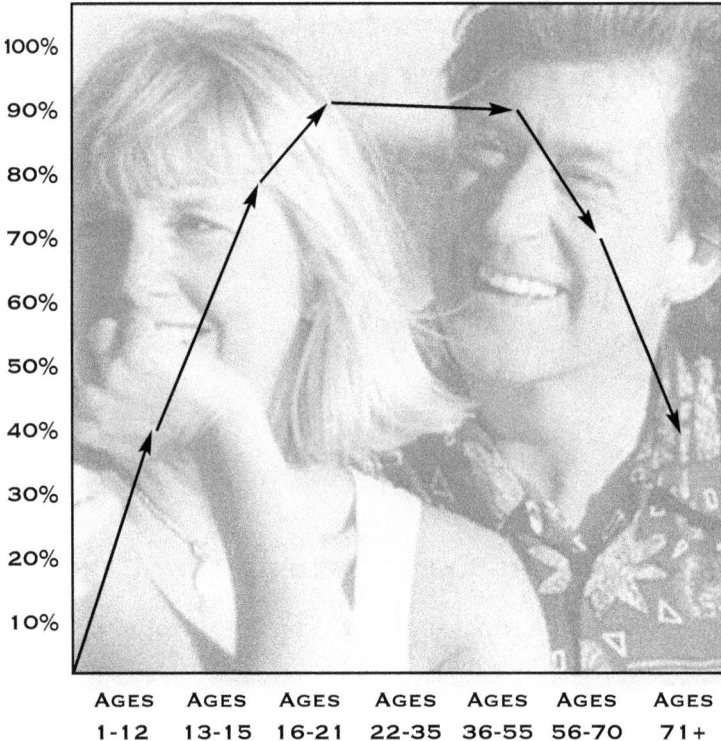

| | AGES 1-12 | AGES 13-15 | AGES 16-21 | AGES 22-35 | AGES 36-55 | AGES 56-70 | AGES 71+ |

As evidenced above, pre-Viagra men began lying less to the women in their lives during Phases VI and VII, coinciding with the time many men experienced at least some erection dysfunction issues. Men, of course, still routinely lied to women when convenient, but certainly less than earlier in their lives when they were at the peak of their sexual prowess.

Twelve years after Viagra, Cialis, Levitra, and a host of generic erection enhancing drugs became universally available, the lying probability curve for men fifty-six and older had been dramatically altered:

PROBABILITY CURVE 2009

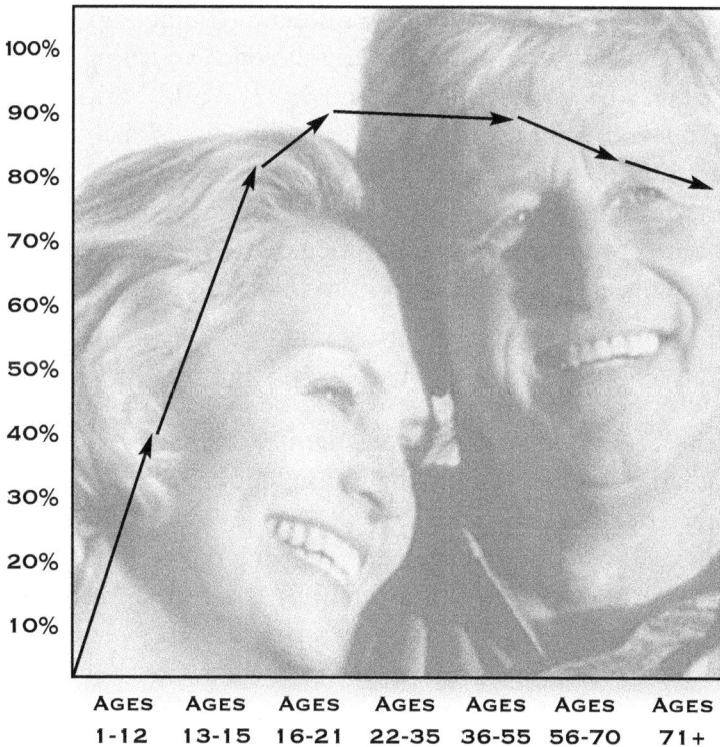

AGES 1-12	AGES 13-15	AGES 16-21	AGES 22-35	AGES 36-55	AGES 56-70	AGES 71+

Confidence in their ability to perform sexually dramatically increased the percentage of time older men felt the need to lie to the women around them.

Back when Viagra was first introduced, men were reluctant to admit trying the product. By 2010, however, older men discuss sexual performance enhancement drugs right along with their favorite sports statistics. The most common *gag gift* at bachelor parties for older guys is a supply of a performance enhancing drug, usually accompanied by a card that says *good 'til your last drop.*

THOMAS CLARK, 56, DISCOVERS VIAGRA

Wednesday, October 27, 1999 was a day Thomas Clark would long remember. As a Coca-Cola Vice President, Thomas was at Yankee Stadium as a guest of the baseball commissioner, watching his beloved Atlanta Braves try to stay alive in the 1999 World Series. It was an exceptionally cool evening, made colder by his Braves' inability to score runs. Clark was in a suite with other Coke VPs and several of their largest customers, drinking adult beverages rather than his company's products.

"Hey, Clark! You might as well pay me now," Ms. Patty Brown said to him. "My Yankees are gonna wrap it up tonight! Gonna be a long trip home for you Braves fans!"

"It's not over yet, damn it! We're gonna score some runs this inning," Thomas retorted. Immediately, he wished he hadn't used "damn." Even though the group was mostly men, there were half a dozen women present. Clark's southern upbringing caused him to act more reserved in the presence of ladies.

Everyone was whooping it up, really enjoying the evening, though the Yankees were up three games to none in the series. "Tell you what Tommy-boy," Patty said. "I'll make it easy on you! If your Braves score more than three runs even in a Yankee sweep, our bet's off! But if we hold 'em to two runs or less you gotta pay me our $100 bet and take me for a steak after the game! You on?"

"Yup! This is the inning we're gonna turn it around," Thomas declared. *Man, we better win! Taking Patty's group for steaks will cost me an arm and a leg here in New York! Or did she mean just the two of us? Uh-oh!*

Going into the top of the ninth the Yankees were up four to one over the Braves. "Just three more little old outs, Tommy-boy! I can taste that steak already!" Patty licked her lips and looked Thomas up and down as

WHY MEN MUST LIE

she spoke.

The Braves went down in twelve pitches; the Yankees had swept the series. "Pay me and take me," Patty said. "I mean to dinner of course!" With all the pandemonium in the ball park, only Thomas heard her tease.

This is gonna be tricky. "Okay, you win! Should we wait for that steak until you and your team are visiting Atlanta?" Thomas asked Patty.

"Team? It's just you and me, baby! And I'm starving! We're going right over to the Manhattan Cafe!"

Patty Brown was the Vice President of Purchasing for one of Coke's largest retail customers. She'd been teasing Thomas for years, but tonight she had that look in her eye.

Thomas felt trapped, but it was his own fault. "Okay, Ms. Brown! Let's go!"

The Manhattan Café was beyond packed, but the maîtred' knew Ms. Brown. He put them back in a corner booth with the most privacy of any in the restaurant. "Ain't this cozy," Patty said. "Guess it helped that I tipped him the $100 bill I just won from you. Now, you gotta buy me the biggest filet on the menu and a double Ketel One martini with anchovy olives. What are you drinking, Tommy dear?"

"Uh, I better just have a Coke."

"No way! I'm the customer and I demand you drink with me! Bring him what I'm having," Patty told the waiter. "And be quick about it! We're celebrating!"

When the waiter left, Thomas said to Patty, "Lots of fun tonight, but I don't want to keep you out too late. Didn't you come on the company plane with your staff?"

"Yep, but I'm staying the weekend right here in New York. If you're not good, I'll just go over and meet with the Pepsi folks tomorrow. I bet they'd be happy to see me. Tonight, Mr. Coca-Cola, you're mine."

Oh, Shit! Now what do I do? Patty Brown had met Thomas's wife on several occasions. Clearly, that didn't matter to Patty.

"Hey, Tommy-boy, you still pluggin' that little girl down in advertising?" Patty asked.

"What?"

"You heard me, sweetheart! You think nobody knows about you and

Jill? Get real! I'm not that much older than her! And I've got bigger tits!"

Thomas Clark's world had just gotten rocked. *Oh, brother! I'm in big trouble here!*

"Would you excuse me? I need to use the men's room. Be right back," Thomas said.

"Go ahead and tell your wife good night, Tommy-boy! And hurry back!"

As soon as Clark was out of sight Patty poured two finely ground Viagra tablets into his martini. *Give him just a little help,* she thought.

"Bottom's up on that Ketel, sweetie! I want a glass of cabernet with my steak!" she said.

By the time Patty and Thomas got back to the Plaza Hotel, it was one am. "Nightcap in the Oak Room," she said.

Though tired from the long day, Thomas was surprised at how aroused he was getting. He'd never thought of Patty as all that attractive, but she seemed to be getting him pretty excited. Or was she really just teasing him?

After one quick drink Patty said, "Your room or mine, Tommy-boy? Looks to me like you're good and ready!"

The next morning, Patty had breakfast delivered to their room. Over coffee she said, "So, pretty good, huh? Not too bad for an old broad if I do say so myself! Looks like you don't need any breakfast! Come on over here! Guess that Viagra I gave you is to your liking."

"What?"

"I wanted to make sure we didn't waste our night, so I put a Viagra in your martini. Don't tell me you didn't notice!"

"What?"

"If you say 'what' again I'm switching to Pepsi! Just shut-up and enjoy," Patty said.

"You shouldn't have done that! What if it would've hurt me?"

"Don't be so dramatic! All guys your age should use it! Makes you rise and shine like when you were young! We can do it again after breakfast. Then I gotta run!"

When Thomas told me about his first experience with Viagra, he had just retired from Coke. "How'd she know about Jill?" I asked. "Did your wife ever find out?"

"If she did she never brought it up. When I was saying good-bye to Patty she handed me two more Viagra and said, 'So you won't disappoint Mary Beth when you get home! See ya!' I got myself a prescription and been using them ever since. You know, it's the drug that made Pfizer famous. I wish Coke's drug prescription plan covered it!"

RICHARD HANNIGAN, 57, SILENT LYING

Richard Hannigan was reanalyzing his company's early retirement option for about the hundredth time. It really was a very attractive offer. In fact, working another couple of years just didn't make financial sense now that his employer would equalize his pension and Social Security as though he had waited until he was sixty-five to retire. Richard and Ellen had no debt, and the kids were all doing well on their own. Just one problem: how could he possibly be with Ellen 24/7 for the rest of his life?

For the past twenty or so years, Hannigan's wife had fantasized about buying a motor home and seeing the sights of North America when he retired. Just buy a big, diesel bus and *hit the road*. Ellen had a preliminary list of travel destinations that would take several years to complete. Richard had always gone along with Ellen's plans, but he now realized that driving in an RV across America wasn't at all what he wanted to do. Why had he just said "yes, dear" instead of speaking his mind?

In the office that he'd soon be vacating was a picture of him and Ellen taken on their honeymoon in Hawaii. God, Ellen had been gorgeous back then. What a figure! Another more recent photograph taken at a grandchild's baptism was much less appealing. Still relatively pretty, Ellen was fifty pounds heavier than in the first picture. Though she'd made many attempts to lose weight, those extra pounds just wouldn't go away. Ellen's passion was reading and her appetite for books went hand-in-hand with her appetite for bakery goods, especially cookies. She knew every convection oven option in the various motor coaches they had considered purchasing.

Richard refocused his attention on the retirement papers. *Hell, I'll have more spendable income if I retire than if I continue to work! Guess I have to tell Ellen about the company's offer.*

At home that evening Richard mixed himself a tall martini and prepared to discuss early retirement with his wife. Ellen sat down in front of him with her glass of wine and said, "Richard, there's something we have to talk about."

Surprised, Richard said, "Really? Well, I was going to talk to you about something too, but you go first."

"You know, Richard, we haven't made love in a very long time. Now don't interrupt me. I need to get this out! Please, just listen. It's been nearly a year since you showed any interest in being intimate. I know I've gained weight and I know that's a turn off for you, but you just show no interest at all."

Has it been that long? Guess it has. Where's this going?

"Richard, I've been going to the gym to try to get back in shape and, well, I met someone there. He's a little older than me, but he loves me, Richard. And he shows interest in me all the time. He's a widower and he wants me to go away with him. Now. I'm very, very sorry to tell you like this, but I just feel you don't really care to be with me anymore. Say something."

I can't believe I'm hearing this! Is this possible? "Have you slept with him yet?" Richard asked.

"I tell you I may leave you, and all you want to know is 'have you slept with him?' Christ Richard, is that how you see everything? In terms of sex? You haven't been interested in sex with me! What do you care?"

"Ellen, it's a fair question. Have you slept with him? Yes or no?" Richard asked.

"Yes, damn it! I have!" Ellen started crying, but she held her ground.

"You love him, then, Ellen?"

"I guess I do! He's got a new motor coach and he wants me to just leave everything and go with him. Richard, he wants me to marry him, right away. I'm truly sorry, but it's what I want to do. Can you forgive me? Please?"

I think I just died and went to heaven! Holy Christ, I must be the luckiest bastard in the world!

"Richard, say something!" Ellen pleaded.

Flash: "I don't know what to say, Ellen. You've just explained to me that you want to leave me for another man. That you've slept with him already. What can I say?" Richard managed to look truly hurt.

"It's what I want, Richard. I'm sorry, I truly am. You just haven't cared for a very long time."

If I handle this just right, I won't have to split my retirement with her! I can go rock and roll! I've gotta be real careful how I play this.

Flash: "Ellen, if it's what you really want then all I can do is try to get on with my life. It'll be really hard, but you've made your decision. What do you want me to do? If you're leaving, I guess I'll try to sell the house and get an apartment. What else can I do?"

Thank God she spoke first. Now I can retire and do what I want to do!

"Thank you for being reasonable, Richard. I don't want anything, really. John, that's his name, John, has everything. He says if you'll be reasonable and give me a quick divorce there's no reason to ask for anything."

"When do you plan to leave?" Richard asked.

"Well, telling you was the hard part. I've already spoken with our family attorney and told him all I want is out. I'm leaving now, tonight. I've got four big suitcases packed upstairs. If you could just help me get them down to the garage and in my car, I'd like to just go."

"Now? Just like that?" Richard said. "What will we tell our daughters?"

"Richard, I already told them. They weren't that surprised. It's better this way. You know and I know that you'll be angry after it's sunk in. Please, just help me with the luggage. Let's part friends."

Fifteen minutes later Ellen gave her husband of thirty-five years a kiss on the cheek and drove away to start her new life with John. Richard went back in his house and downed his martini. Then he mixed a second one. It was the happiest day of his life.

Richard Hannigan's story is a clear example of another form of dishonesty that I heard many confidants describe, Silent Lying. Men in Phases VI and VII told many stories of how they had been completely dishonest with their wives by never saying what they were truly thinking and feeling. Silent lying often escalates over the course of a relationship to the point where a man detests everything about his life, but never voices his true feelings to his partner.

Richard hadn't told Ellen that the last thing he wanted to do when he retired was drive around the country in a motor home. He felt only relief when his wife announced that she had another man. Richard kept his sweetened retirement package to himself and described his state of mind as *euphoric*.

DIRK JOHNSON, 59, DON'T NEED THE BIG V IF YOU ADOPT THE BIG C

A theme I heard again and again from men in Phases V, VI, and VII was best epitomized by a yacht salesman at the Miami Boat Show. Dirk Johnson was a retired insurance executive who had taken on a second career selling expensive boats. Dirk worked hard to look ten years younger than his age. He had the perfect Florida tan and was an outrageous flirt. Women found him extremely attractive.

Dirk delivered a sixty-foot yacht to one of my friends at the boat show and attended the owners orientation cruise to help explain the operational requirements of the new craft. Dirk then hosted an elaborate dinner party at one of the hottest restaurants in town to celebrate the sale, and his six figure commission.

After the dinner and several rounds of after-dinner drinks, Dirk engaged in a conversation with five women who were seated at a table next to our party.

"May I buy you ladies a round of drinks to apologize for our loud and obnoxious male behavior during dinner?" Dirk asked.

"Well, you certainly should!" one of the women responded. "You gentlemen have been behaving like teenagers for the last hour and a half! What are you celebrating?"

"Two things, really," Dirk said. "I just delivered a beautiful new sixty-foot Tiara Yacht to Tim over there, and us guys have been drinking to being alive and capable at our advancing ages!"

"Wow! That must have been a big commission check for you," said another one of the ladies, who obviously understood the yachting industry and the price of a Tiara. "What do you mean 'alive and capable at your ages'?"

That was exactly the response Dirk had hoped for. "You know, capable of getting it up without Viagra!"

All five women howled with laughter at Dirk's statement. "Come on," the first woman said. "All guys your age use Viagra to make you think you're still twenty-one! Who do you think you're kidding? We're all married, we know men!"

"Well, maybe that's why you don't believe me," Dirk responded. "If you've all been married to the same men for a long time, maybe they need Viagra. But that doesn't apply to guys like us!"

"What are you talking about? Are you inferring that our husbands need Viagra because they're married to us? How dare you!"

"Not because they're married to you women specifically! Because they're married, period," Dirk said.

"Now you have to explain yourself!" the woman who'd first spoken to Dirk said. "What do you mean?"

"You sure you want me to answer that?" Dirk asked. "I mean, I'll give you ladies an honest explanation if you really want me to, but you probably won't like it."

He had their undivided attention.

"Okay. I'm not going to pull any punches. Here's how it is. If a man is excited by a new female conquest, it invigorates him. Makes him feel truly young again. Nine times out of ten that man won't need any *help* because he's excited like when he was a boy. A man doesn't always need the big V, sometimes he just needs the big C, change. If a man's truly *turned on* by the prospects of a new partner, he usually rises to the occasion, if you'll pardon the pun," Dirk concluded.

Silence befell both tables. Dirk's male guests were all embarrassed by his brazen conversation with a group of women he'd just met. The women seemed to all be truly contemplating what Dirk had said. After several minutes one of the women asked, "Are you serious? Any new female partner can usually cause that reaction? Just because it's something different?"

"That's exactly what I'm saying, Dear. Men are sexual animals. They need new stimulation from time to time. Otherwise, they need Viagra."

The five women finished the drinks that Dirk had bought them and left. There weren't any affectionate *good-byes.*

"Christ, Johnson! You embarrassed them and us! Don't you know better than to tell women the truth?"

"Of course I do! But sometimes I just can't help myself!" Dirk said.

Many confidants fifty and older told stories about how they *re-discovered* their sexual vitality when *re-excited* by a different female partner. It seemed to make little difference if the new partner was old or young, attractive or average. Someone different, a *change* seemed to make all the difference for a majority of men.

LYLE SHORT, 60, LIFE OFF THE ROAD

Phase VI men describe *First Flash Reactions* that are sometimes less intense, but still the dominant influence in all relationships with females. They continue to see every woman they encounter in terms of her sexual desirability, but the concept of consequences begins to affect men's lying behavior far more than when they were younger.

Men under fifty feel invincible. They believe they can fix anything they screw up, or at least lie their way out of situations with minimal long-term affect. Men fifty-six and older begin to experience twangs of doubt about their ability to recover from their mistakes and are, therefore, way more careful about their lying.

Lyle Short had been *living on the road* his entire career. After earning a master's degree in economics, Lyle had gone to work for a German bank that sent him all over the globe to evaluate investment opportunities. Though he continued to be based in the bank's offices in New York City, Lyle had averaged more than 200 nights a year in hotel rooms over his thirty-five years with the bank. Lyle had received numerous promotions, but now the bank wanted him to accept a senior VP slot that would have him home in NYC virtually every night until he retired.

Lyle's wife, Jenny, was thrilled that her husband would finally be *like a real person* at home with her every night. Lyle knew that being *grounded* would completely alter the lifestyle he had come to cherish. Lyle Short had girlfriends in cities all over the world. Some of these relationships had lasted many years; others were more opportunistic *short duration* affairs. Now Lyle was stuck in New York with no excuse to be gone overnight.

"Isn't this wonderful, dear? No more packing and unpacking. Finally, we can have a normal life." Jenny was genuinely thrilled with Lyle's new position.

Flash: "Yes, honey, it'll be great." I can't do this! I'll go nuts! Why now? I won't make it to retirement.

"We can do all the things you never had time to do. Weekends in New England or at the shore. Just you and me!" Jenny was ecstatic. "And you won't always be tired! We can make love like when we were kids!"

Lyle watched his wife literally bubbling over with joy and anticipation. Jenny had maintained her slim figure and girlish good looks. She could easily pass for forty-five instead of fifty-nine. A petite woman, Jenny still wore size four dresses.

"You're a very beautiful woman, Jenny," Lyle told his wife.

Flash: "I hope I can live up to your expectations, now that I'll be home all the time."

For the next six months Jenny kept Lyle busy with weekend trips and nights on Broadway, catching up for all the years her husband had been on the road. Jenny bought new lingerie and cooked candlelight dinners at home. She bleached her hair a lighter blond and prepared every evening for Lyle's return from the office, greeting him at the door with a radiant smile. The happier Jenny became, the more miserable was Lyle.

After one year in his *grounded* VP position, Lyle had aged ten years. He'd gained forty pounds and started smoking again after being off cigarettes for twenty-five years.

"Have you been smoking?" Jenny asked one evening as she greeted Lyle at the door.

Flash: "Uh, no, dear. The cab I got in was filled with smoke. Must've absorbed it in my suit. What are we doing for dinner?"

"I fixed us a wonderful salad with smoked salmon and candied pecans. You'll love it. And I opened a fantastic white Bordeaux."

"I need a big martini first," Lyle said.

"Honey, you really should cut down on the martinis. I'm worried that you're putting on a little weight," Jenny said.

"One Goddamn martini is not gonna kill me!" Lyle snapped.

"Lyle, what's wrong? I just thought maybe the vodka would keep you from enjoying the wine. Are you okay, honey?" Jenny was fighting back the tears.

Flash: "Sorry. Just had a rough day, that's all. Didn't mean to take it out on you."

"That's okay, dear. I know it's hard for you being stuck in an office every day. Do you miss traveling, honey?"

Flash: "Hell no! I mean, no, just sometimes I feel cooped up, I guess."

"Maybe we should take a trip to Europe, dear. You know, stay in one of those fancy hotels you liked so much! Wouldn't that be fun?"

"Yeah, maybe. Let me think about it," Lyle said. *Wonder if I could sneak in a couple of visits to Giselle or Ingrid. That might save my life!*

"Here's your martini, dear!"

Lyle and Jenny spent the following April traveling in France and Germany. Under the guise of "visiting old friends at bank offices," Lyle was able to reconnect with a few of his old girlfriends while Jenny shopped.

The Shorts spent April in Europe each of the next ten years.

I caught up with Lyle at the retirement dinner of a mutual friend. He was near his seventieth birthday. As Jenny Short table-hopped to talk to her friends, I asked him, "Still traveling to Europe every year? Still have afternoons free while Jenny shops?"

"It's the only reason I'm still alive! Thank Christ some of my girlfriends were twenty years younger than me when I met them! They still look damn good!" Lyle said.

"Jenny never gets suspicious? You've gotten away with it all these years?"

"I'm a damn fine liar!" Short said. "Not to you guys, of course, just to women!"

Lawrence Middleton, 62, Coping with Tragedy

Friends of mine with whom I shared draft versions of *Why Men Must Lie* advised against including chapters that dealt with death. Some of the most revealing personal experiences related to me were, however, about men's personal tragedies. For men in Phases VI and VII, suffering the loss of a spouse causes self-evaluation that provides remarkable insight into men's true characters.

The death of a wife was, by far, the experience men found most difficult to discuss. Only a few of my confidants shared revelations about their most personal feelings concerning loss. Many, however, needed to talk about their lives as unexpectedly single men after the death of their spouses. To omit such stories seemed somehow dishonest.

Lawrence Middleton had only two jobs in his life. He served in the US Air Force for eight years and then, at age twenty-six, he went to work for the postal service in his home town of San Francisco, California. After thirty-six years as a letter carrier, Larry was all set to retire. His route had kept him in amazingly good physical condition. He was often told he looked fifteen years younger than sixty-two.

This made his wife, Edith, both proud and a little envious. She too was near retirement from the post office with the same amount of seniority as her husband, though she was seven years younger. While Larry had chosen to remain in mail delivery, Edith had advanced through the system and was the postmaster of the downtown San Francisco sorting facility. She was, in fact, Larry's boss. All the postal system personnel teased Edith that she had *robbed the cradle* when she married Larry because he looked so much younger than she did.

Edith and Larry had managed to purchase a townhouse in downtown San Francisco before property values sky-rocketed. It was now worth nearly two million dollars. Their townhouse had long been paid off. They intended to take retirement, sell their over-valued home, and move to a less expensive inland location that would enable them to live the *good life* with ease.

Three months prior to their mutual retirement date, Edith died of a heart attack right at her desk in the post office. Unbeknownst to her husband, Edith had purchased government sponsored supplemental life insurance for both of them. Because she died *on the job*, Lawrence Middleton received a totally unexpected two million dollars from Edith's life insurance. Additionally, he was entitled to a substantial portion of her retirement pay for the rest of his life. Larry found himself widowed, retired, relatively rich, and totally lost.

I met Larry at *poker night* as a guest of Middleton's next door neighbor. The following morning we all went for coffee at the local Starbucks.

"Good morning, Larry. I think you were the big winner last night."

"Yeah, I guess I was. We had a lot of fun, huh? What did you think of your buddy's poker club?" Larry asked.

"Good group of guys! I was honored to sit in. But it would have been more fun if you hadn't won all my money!"

Larry laughed, "Dumb luck, I assure you! Where'd you say you were from?"

"Naples, Florida. Came out to San Francisco to visit some old army buddies. I guess the friends you make when you're young and in the service always hold a place in your heart. Couple of them came all the way back east to attend my wife's funeral last year. That meant a lot to me."

"I'm sorry to hear about your wife. Mine died two years ago and I'm still sort of in shock, I guess," Larry said.

"Yeah, Frank mentioned that to me, so I wasn't afraid to open up the subject. I don't know what I would've done without Frank and some of the guys to talk to back then. How are you doing with the loss?"

"How long were you married?" Larry asked.

"Twenty-two years. How about you?"

"My whole life, it felt like. Married Edith while I was still in the Air Force. I was twenty-five, she was eighteen, so thirty-seven years we were together. And I mean really together! We both went to work in the same post office here when I got out of the service. Never had kids, although we sure tried. She went to college and did well in the postal system. She was the postmaster where I worked. She was my boss!" Larry said.

"That's a lot of togetherness. Sounds like it worked out well."

To my great surprise, Larry said, "Yes and no."

"That's a bit of an odd answer, Larry. Care to elaborate?"

"Want another latte? If you got time, I'll tell you about it."

Seated against the back wall in Starbucks, Larry began his story.

"I met Edith in a bar about a year before I got out of the service. She was this cute young thing out with a bunch of her girlfriends. Guess she liked my uniform. I'd come home to San Francisco on leave from Nellis Air Force Base in Nevada for two weeks and we just hit it off. Next thing I knew she was visiting me in Las Vegas once a month. When my second hitch was over, I got out and came back here. We both got jobs in the post office. We moved in together, but that upset her folks, so we got married. Edith wanted kids and tried to get pregnant, but she just never did.

"After a couple years Edith's parents loaned us the money to put down on a run-down old town house. We fixed it up real nice and paid it off in fifteen years. Damn thing's worth nearly two million dollars now!

"I liked being outside in the fresh air, so I just kept carryin' the mail. Edie went to college and went right up the ranks in the postal system. She'd given up trying to have a kid, and put all her energy into her career. Before you knew it, twenty years went by."

"Larry, did you want kids?"

"Not really. I mean, it would've been okay, but it wasn't all that important to me. 'Bout the time Edie turned fifty and I was fifty-seven, though, life sort of caught up with us," Larry said.

"What do you mean, *caught up* with you? Don't mean to pry, but you seem saddened by your own words, Larry."

"Well, to tell you the truth I guess we were both just about bored to death. We had good, secure jobs. Edie made twice what I did, of course, and we'd paid off the townhouse. All we did was go to work and go out to eat. Tough on Edie because she started putting on weight, while I stayed thin 'cause of all the walkin' on the job. We were sitting in this neighborhood restaurant one night just finishing eating and two half undressed young beauties walked by on the way to the lady's. One of them smiled at me and said 'hi.' Never saw her before in my life."

"'Who was that?' Edie asked.

"No idea," I said.

"Well, she certainly knew you!" my wife told me.

"Uh-oh. That's hard to get past!" I commented.

"Tell me about it!" Larry said. "On the way back to their table she did it again! This time, Edith got really mad! 'Who is that bitch?' she asked. 'I swear I've never seen her before in my life!' I said. Edith didn't speak to me for three days! We'd get up, have coffee just like every day for the past thirty years, and walk to the post office. Come home after work, eat, whatever, and not one word for three damn days!

"Finally, on Friday of that week, Edith spoke. 'If you don't tell me about that bitch I'm leaving!' she said. I got really pissed off at my wife for the first time in thirty-two years. Said some things I shouldn't have said."

"Wow, Larry. Maybe we should just drop this subject."

"No! I need to tell somebody! It's been eating at me for seven years! I said some really dumb things."

"Okay, like what?"

"Like, 'if you hadn't gained thirty pounds, maybe I wouldn't have noticed her.' That kind of thing. I didn't want it to sound as mean as it did, but once I'd said it, I was truly screwed. Edith stayed at her mother's house for two weeks. She lost about ten pounds while she was there. She called me up on that third weekend and said she wanted to talk. I said, 'Come on back home and we'll straighten all this out.' She was back in less than an hour."

"When Edith walked back into our house she said, 'I have three questions. If you will tell me the absolute truth, everything will be fine. I'll know if you're not telling me the truth, so please don't lie. And don't hold back. I want you to be honest with me like you've never been before!'"

"I said, 'What do you mean, honest like I've never been before? I haven't ever lied to you!' Edith said, 'But you've never told me everything! Will you answer my three questions?'"

"I said, 'Okay, I'll try. What are your three questions?'"

Edith said, "Please listen to all three before you try to answer. First, did it matter to you that I couldn't have children? Second, from the time you met me right up until now, did you ever want to have sex with another woman? Last, do you really love me enough to spend the rest of our lives together?"

For several minutes, Larry sat and stared into his coffee. Finally, he continued, "My friend, I was scared. I sensed that she somehow already knew the answers to those three questions far better than I did."

"Are you willing to share your answers with a relative stranger?"

"I guess I need to, really," he said. "I told her that having children was never very important to me. I said I'd never even considered having sex with another woman and that I absolutely loved her and wanted nothing more than to be with her forever. She moved back home and our lives returned more or less to the way they had been before."

"So it all worked out okay? That's great."

"Not really. I didn't tell her the truth. I told her what I thought she wanted to hear. The only thing I told her that was really true was that it didn't matter about kids. I never wanted kids. Could have cared less," Larry said. "I'd had several affairs. Some with women right there in the post office. And my life with Edith was convenient; nothing more. Should I have really told her the truth?"

Larry's question to a man he'd just met the night before at a poker game seemed sincere, if a bit odd. Of course, it was a question only he could answer. Several men in Phase VI voiced emotions similar to that expressed by Larry Middleton. A lifetime of lying to their wives caused some men consternation later in life, but seldom actual regret.

As we exited Starbucks, Larry introduced me to an extremely attractive *thirty-something* woman who'd come to meet him for lunch. "Hey, stick around for next week's game and try to win your money back!" he advised. "Rachel here has lots of girlfriends!"

MAX HOWARD, 64, SOCIAL SECURITY BLUES

Turning fifty causes many men to worry that life is more than half over. They reflect on their repressed desires and often give in to *First Flash Reactions* before it's too late even though they previously resisted such behavior. Applying for Social Security, however, removes any doubt that old age is at hand. Nearly every confidant expressed *shock and awe* when they received that first check from the government, their proof in hand that it's time to stop *putting things off.*

Max Howard remembered everything about the day he went to the mailbox and retrieved his first Social Security check. His wife Janet, nine years his junior, still taught school, so Max was home alone to reflect on just what that check meant.

"It was a beautiful late fall day in New Hampshire," Max told a group of his buddies as they sat looking out at Lake Winnipesaukee from the deck of his Cruisers Yacht. "I was feeling great! I'd taken an early morning walk after Janet left for school and the stock market was up a percent and a half at 11:00 am. Of course I knew I'd be getting my first check at some point; hell, I'd filled the forms out six weeks prior! But when I opened that brown US Treasury envelope and saw the $1,856 amount, it hit me! I'm old! I'd been denying that reality ever since I sold my business, but there was the proof!

"I remembered what the girl at the Social Security office advised me, 'better go ahead and start collecting now, Mr. Howard. Statistically, you'll collect more than if you wait 'til seventy, but there are no guarantees, you know.' I just sat there staring at the check thinking 'How long have I got?' 'How long will I be healthy enough to do what I want to do?' More importantly, 'What the hell do I really want to do that I've been putting off all these years?'

"Janet was all wound up in teaching issues and going to visit the grandkids down in Boston. I'd go with her sometimes, but talking to four and six year-olds didn't excite me. So what did excite me? Same thing that had all my life. A nice, slim waist surrounded by big boobs and a round backside!"

That brought a series of *Amens!* and *Right Ons* from the men on his boat.

Max continued, "So I think to myself, 'What's the best way to see some nice female forms nearly all the time?' Answer was easy! Buy a boat! Put it on Winnipesaukee in the summers and take it down the intercoastal to Florida in the fall. Live right on the boat!"

"But you'd never even owned a boat, had you Max?" a buddy asked.

"No, but I'd always wanted one! When Janet got home from school, I had it all figured out! I said, 'Janet, I'm gonna buy a boat!' She said, 'Like hell you are! I want to teach at least three more years and then move to

Boston to be near the kids and grandkids. Besides, you know nothing about boats! Why would you want to learn about 'em at your age?'

I knew at that moment I'd been living a lie for forty years! I'd worked my ass off in my business and given Janet and the kids everything they wanted. Now it was my time! 'Janet,' I said, 'I'm buying a boat! A big one! Big enough to live on! Florida in the winter and back up the intracoastal to Winnipesaukee each spring! What do you think?'

Janet said, "I think you're out of your mind! Forget it! I'm not living like some damn boat floozy! You'd better find some twenty year old for that, mister!"

At exactly that moment, Max's current thirty-something boat floozy, Maria, poked her head out from the galley and said, "Any of you guys need anything? I'm going to get some sun up on the front deck, but I'd be happy to freshen your drinks!"

Five minutes later, a bikini-clad Maria served four Bloody Marys and two beers to Max's friends as she made her way forward.

"Enjoy!" Maria said.

After a moment of silence as the men watched Maria squeeze her way along the port side railing toward the forward deck, Max resumed his story. "I said, 'Janet, that's exactly what I'm gonna do!' She actually laughed! That was four years ago. I think she's still teaching school!"

"So you divorced her? Must've cost you an arm and a leg!"

"And worth every penny! Yep, been divorced over three years, now. This next fall will be my fourth southbound run down the intracoastal! Any you guys wanna crew for me?" Max asked.

"Hell yes!" all his friends screamed.

"Max, do you ever regret just walking away from forty years of marriage?" a friend asked.

"Only regret is that I waited so long!"

"Do the Social Security checks still remind you of your age?" another buddy inquired.

"Naw, I have 'em direct deposited now! They sort of cover the cost of diesel fuel for the boat!"

Max Howard's story was typical of Phase VI men who had the financial wherewithal to act on their late onset *First Flash Reactions.* Of course, many men simply can't afford to be so cavalier about lifestyle changes. Max received an enthusiastic cheer from the men on his yacht that morning when he said, "You know guys, no man ever died saying, 'I wish I'd been more truthful and had less fun!'"

HARRY GILES, 66, OUT THE DOOR AND MORE

Ages forty, fifty, fifty-five and sixty are all traumatic turning points for most men. Nothing, however, drives home a man's diminishing opportunities like forced retirement at age sixty-five. Nearly every Phase VI man I ever listened to talked about retirement sooner or later. Those who were approaching retirement expressed anxiety and apprehension about the dramatic lifestyle change they were contemplating. Men who were already retired, however, told some of the most character-revealing stories I heard.

Harry Giles was both a lawyer and a certified public accountant (CPA). He'd joined one of the *big* eight public accounting firms right out of law school and stayed with it forty years. His firm had an unyielding rule that partners must retire on or before their sixty-sixth birthday. For Harry, forced retirement had been a true revelation.

I met Harry at a financial seminar a few weeks after his retirement party. During an afternoon break, one of the attendees said, "Gee, Mr. Giles, I'm surprised you feel the need to attend this seminar. You must've been exposed to all sorts of financial planning throughout your career. Are you learning much from these kids?"

It was a running joke among the forty or so participants that the average age of the *kids* teaching the financial seminar was about the age of their grandchildren. Harry responded, "You know, I really am. There are so many new financial products it's hard to keep up. I plan on living another thirty years, so I've got to make my money last."

"So you figure you have one third of your life ahead of you after retirement? That's pretty optimistic, isn't it?" The man who'd asked Harry this question was the youngest person attending the seminar.

"Young man," Harry began, "if I remember correctly you stated your age as fifty-three when we did our initial introductions. Is that correct?"

"Uh, yeah. That's right. Pretty good memory if you still recall my age."

"Tell you what. If you guys are interested, after today's session I'll buy a round of drinks and explain exactly why I'm so optimistic," Harry said.

There were five men, all relative strangers who'd met at the seminar, standing in the group when Giles made his drink offer; all showed up in the hotel cocktail lounge at the end of the day.

"Looks like everybody showed up for a free drink. Let's grab that table in the corner and order up. Like I promised, drinks are on me," Harry said.

A very attractive twenty-something waitress came to take the drink order. She was wearing a tip-inducing blouse revealing ample cleavage. "Hi, gentlemen! What'll you have? One check or separate?"

"One check and I'll take it," Harry said. "Vodka martini, up, with regular olives for me. By the way, how old are you?"

"Excuse me?" the waitress countered.

"It's a straight up question! How old are you, today?" Harry had already established that he was buying the drinks. The waitress quickly calculated that her tip was dependent on playing along.

"Today, sir, I'm twenty-four. How old are you?"

"About thrice that! Take our order, please."

When the waitress walked to the bar, Harry said, "I believe I agreed to explain to you gentlemen why I am optimistic enough to believe that I have one third of my life ahead of me, even though I just retired at age sixty-six. It's really quite simple. Over the past forty-eight years I was either getting my education or working my ass off seventy to eighty hours a week helping other people make financial successes of their lives. Oh, I had some fun along the way, but, really, I mostly just toiled away, letting life slip on by. Fortunately, I'm in pretty good health and I've got sufficient investments to live comfortably as long as I don't get stupid or lazy with my money. By lazy, I mean not maximizing my returns; that's why I've met you nice guys here at the seminar."

The waitress served the first round and Harry said, "Back these up with another round, Dear. Okay guys, as to why I'm optimistic that a third of my life's ahead of me: I intend to live every day for the rest of my life as though it's the last day of my life. I'm going to pack thrity years of fun into however much time I have left. So, whether it's two years or twenty I'm gonna get at least thrity years worth of pleasure during my remaining time. Get it?"

"Well, I think I understand your concept, Mr. Giles," said one of the younger guys. "But I'm not sure I understand why you seem to need to 'catch up' on fun. Do you feel your life has really been so disappointing? I mean, did you have so little enjoyment that you feel you wasted your life?"

Again, it was the fifty-three year old who asked Harry these questions that, frankly, made the other men a bit uncomfortable. The questions seemed almost too personal given that the six men had met just three days earlier.

After a longer than normal pause, Harry said, "In a word, yes! I put together a successful career, raised a family, lived a *good* life, but I was completely dishonest about nearly every aspect of my existence. I lived the life that others expected of me; not the life I wanted. Does any of this strike a chord with any of you gentlemen? Am I the only man at the table who feels this way?"

Four of Harry's five guests kept their eyes down, refusing to respond. "Mr. Giles, I've heard other men describe quite similar post-retirement sentiments over the years, but you have been amazingly candid with five relative strangers," I said. "I would imagine that most men experience at least some of the feelings you have been brave enough to voice, but few of us are willing to speak up with such candor."

"I suspect you are correct. I've told you my plan in gross terms, now let me elaborate. On my last day at the office, I suddenly felt a most amazing sense of freedom. 'I don't have to pretend anymore,' I thought. 'I don't have to try to be somebody I'm not!'" Harry said.

"In the three weeks since I retired, I've ordered a new Ferrari, quit my stuffy-ass golf club where I've been a member for twenty-five years, and resigned from the Republican Party. I'm never setting foot in a church again, and I'm damn sure never going to another opera or symphony! Two weeks ago I met a gorgeous woman in a bar and had sex with her that night! First good sex I've had since before I got married! Actually, I came to this seminar partly so I could stay in this swanky hotel and get drunk at the bar if I feel like it! And look around for another good piece!"

The second round of drinks arrived just as Harry said "And look around for another good piece!"

The waitress said, "Well, the action picks up around here about 7 when the band starts, so you're in the right place, sir!"

The men sipped their second drinks, absorbing all that Harry had said. Finally, one of them asked, "Harry, I believe you told us during introductions that you are married. What does your wife think of all this?"

"Now, just why in the hell would you think I'd tell her any of this?" Harry asked. "You guys want another drink?"

Harry's story was not that atypical of Phase VI men who'd 'walked the straight and narrow' as required of them by their careers only to finally experience personal freedom after retirement. That Harry could be perfectly candid with a group of men he'd only just met while remaining totally incapable of being truthful with his wife is also pretty normal.

Harry is an 'associate' I've maintained contact with over the years. He's already packed at least thrity years of 'pleasure' into the twelve years since he retired. And yes, he's still married.

BOB BARNES, 69, LOOKING OVER THE EDGE INTO OLD AGE

Recently, much has been made about the concept of re-evaluating aging. People like to think that *sixty is the new forty* and that *eighty is the new sixty*. Whether or not this *new aging* has any real validity remains to be seen, but the concept is certainly popular with older people. It has been reported that men over fifty are now undergoing nearly the same number of facelifts as women over fifty, further evidence that mature individuals of both sexes want to believe that *new aging* is real.

I was recently reacquainted with Bob Barnes at a popular watering hole in Naples, Florida. Several years before we had been paired up in the same foursome at a charity golf event, after which Barnes had entertained the golfers with stories from his very colorful life.

"So, Bob, what have you been up to over the past few years?" I asked him over a drink.

"How much time you got? I've completely reinvented myself since I last saw you! Notice anything different about me?" Bob asked.

"Well, not really. You have a great tan and look super healthy! That's always good."

"Anything else?"

"Uh, no."

"Christ! I had a face lift! Cost me eighty-thousand dollars! Also, had some hair transplanted! I'm determined to stay young," Bob said. "Lost maybe twenty pounds since that tournament at the Vineyards. You know what that means!"

"Uh, no, Bob. What does that mean?"

"For Christ's sake! It means I've stopped looking over the edge into old age. I've decided to be young again. I got younger women chasing me all over town. I've hardly got time to sleep!"

"How much younger, Bob?"

"Well, if they're over fifty I just won't talk to 'em. Thirty-five is a good match for a guy my age." At this point in our conversation two rather attractive women sat down on bar stools to Bob's right. He immediately turned his full attention to them.

"Evening ladies. Haven't seen you two here before. Where are you from?" Bob asked.

"Well, we're here for the season from Twin Cities. You're rather forward, aren't you, sir?"

"Sir? Do I look that old? I don't mean to be aggressive, I'm just friendly. May I buy you ladies a drink?"

"No, thank you. We're perfectly capable of buying our own drinks."

Bob Barnes was not deterred.

Flash: "Of course you're capable of buying your own drinks, but I won the Florida lotto two months ago! I'm still celebrating! So, will you ladies please allow the state of Florida to buy your drinks? Think of those drinks as a kind of tax rebate. Bet that'll make 'em taste even better."

"Did you really win the lotto? How much?" The dark haired woman just couldn't help herself; she had to know "how much."

Flash: "Sure did! Netted out after taxes to about six million dollars!"

"Oh my God! I've never met anyone who actually won! I've been playing Powerball and Pix Six back home for years. Were they your numbers or did you let the machine pick them?" the other woman asked.

Flash: "My numbers!" Bob told them. At this point my friend arrived for our dinner date and I said 'good-bye' to Bob and his new friends.

I ran into Bob about three weeks later.

"Hello Bob. How many drinks did buy for those two women from Minnesota?"

"Several, I don't really remember, but I'm still seeing Stella, the blonde. Remember her?"

"Of course. She's very attractive. Bob, did you actually win the lotto?"

"What? Oh hell no! You surely didn't fall for that one did you? Thought you knew better! That story just got my 'foot in the door,' so to speak. But here comes Stella now. She still believes the lotto line, so don't give me away!"

Bob introduced me to Stella.

Flash: "Met this guy when we won a big charity golf tournament a few years back. Do you want to join Stella and me for dinner? We're celebrating my fifty-fifth birthday which is actually tomorrow!"

"Doesn't Bob look young for fifty-five?" Stella said.

"Yes, he sure does. I'll pass on dinner, thanks. Happy birthday."

As Bob and Stella were seated for dinner it occurred to me that Barnes had been sixty-nine at that golf tournament that we, of course, had not won some three years earlier. Barnes had not won the lotto and tomorrow was probably not his birthday, certainly not his fifty-fifth. Bob had *come clean* with a casual male acquaintance about his lies, but continued to lie unashamedly to every woman he met, about absolutely everything.

PHASE VII

AGES 71+

LIVING WITH A LIFE OF LYING

MIKE MCCOY, 71, ONE HOUR A DAY, AND NOT EVERY DAY

Remember Mike McCoy, the confirmed *majority* group bachelor back in Phase V? Mike exhibited an extremely cavalier attitude about lying to women that was representative of nearly all bachelors who confided in me. Frankly, that same cavalier attitude is projected by many men who find themselves *single again* late in life.

Mike turned seventy-one in late 2009 and I met with him again just prior to finalizing *Why Men Must Lie*. Still a very active, health conscious individual, Mike lives in the same Marina Del Mar condo that he bought when he left the SEALS some thirty-five years ago. He still drives a Porsche, and he still likes the ladies.

"Mike, it's great to see you again! You don't look any older than the last time I saw you twenty years ago!"

"Hey! Remember, you're supposed to lie to women, not your old buddies!" Mike responded. "But thanks just the same. I still run on the beach everyday and do everything I can to fight the aging process. And nothing keeps you young like changing girlfriends every so often!"

"So you never got married?"

"Hell no! I told you thirty years ago and again twenty years ago, I'm not cut out for a long-term relationship! Although I will admit I keep 'em longer than I used to!"

"How long now, Mike?"

"Oh, I'm not opposed to up to six months. After that they all get clingy and a little boring. Besides, after that long they figure out you've never told them the truth about anything. That generally pisses 'em off enough to leave. So it all works out in the end."

"Mike, over the years I've repeated what you told us that morning at breakfast in Paris dozens of times! Do you remember, 'Been there, done that?"

"Of course I remember it. I'm old, not senile. Kinda sums up what I just told you, doesn't it? After a man's 'been there, done that' a few months he's just too bored to stay. But an old guy I go to breakfast with has a better one. Name's Brian Worth. He's eighty-four, but spry as hell! Still likes the ladies, but you know what he says to me first thing every morning we get together?" Mike asked.

"No, tell me."

"'Women are good for one hour a day, but not everyday.' Doesn't that just about sum it up? I mean, hell, if you can be with 'em when you want, but do what you want the rest of the time, life's perfect."

"So, Mike, you never came close to getting married? Never tempted even a little?"

"Mister, I'm an honest man. I never tried to do or be something I'm not. Had my share of women, but I always started wishing for a new one after a short while. All men do; I'm just honest about it," he said.

Mike's statement forced this question. "Mike, you just claimed to be an honest man, but you've told me you always lie to women. Isn't that inconsistent?"

"You know as a man that it's not. Women just want things us men never really do want. Women see life totally different. You can't tell a woman what you need all the time, so why pretend? The honorable thing to do is be consistent in your lying. Fact is, if you could go back and talk to all the women I've been with, they'd tell you it's easier to deal with a man like me than a man who'll marry them and then start lying."

Mike remains the poster child of the majority of lifelong bachelors. They feel no compulsion whatsoever to be truthful with women. Or is their total deceit actually easier for women to deal with than most men's combination of Overt, Borderline, and Silent Lying?

JAMES MARSH, 72, CLOSED CIRCUIT LYING

Stories of lying to women told to me by men in Phase VII usually contain an element of personal tragedy. Very often their stories begin with remembrances of losses tapered with traces of guilt, followed by tales of personal recovery as they attempt to find happiness in *mature living*.

I concede to a certain fascination about the stories these older men tell because virtually all of these men mention *being older*, then proceed to describe *First Flash Reactions* to women that mirror those of younger men.

James Marsh was a man who enjoyed working with his hands. As a young man, James had served with an elite team of US Navy divers that specialized in disarming underwater explosives during World War II. He had been decorated for valor and was very active in veterans groups in New England.

James was a master electrician working for a German-owned automobile parts manufacturer when I met him while consulting for the parent company. He had an inborn distrust of consultants and initial interactions between he and I did not go well. Over time, however, James became intrigued by the consulting project's potential and devoted many hours to helping make the project successful. The work often kept us working late into the night so as not to interrupt normal daily production within the factory. During *wait time* between machine installations,

James opened up about his personal life.

"So, James, you've told us that you were in the navy from 1940 through 1946. Did you go to work in this facility right after your discharge?"

"Yup. Been here ever since. Could've retired years ago, but I like what I do. Beats the hell out of sitting around the house every day. Plus, trips to our plants in Germany every so often are really interesting. I've made a lot of friends over there in the last forty-seven years," James told the project team.

"Do you speak German?"

"Yup. Taught myself! I get fooled on a word or two here and there, but basically I get along just fine. I can write it, too." He was justifiably proud of his linguistic capabilities.

One of the younger electricians who had apprenticed under Marsh said, "Go ahead James. Tell him how you really learned your German."

After several moments of silent consideration, Marsh finally said, "I learned it the best way you can. In bed."

This brought quite a chuckle from Marsh's fellow electricians. "James, is there a story there?" I asked.

"Yup. Wanna hear it, you're gonna have to buy the beer when this installation's over."

Later that evening in a local tavern, James opened up. "The first time the company sent me to Germany to see how their electricians did things over there was back in '58. I was in Frankfort on my thirty-fifth birthday and could speak only about ten words of German. But my brother electricians insisted on taking me out to one of their beer halls to celebrate. After five or six steins of that strong German brew, I was feeling pretty tipsy, but they had me singing right along with 'em! All of a sudden this big, strong German woman came over to our table and said 'You American?' I, of course, said 'yes,' and she picked me right up off the bench and said, 'You work tomorrow?'

"It was Saturday night, so I didn't, but I wasn't sure what to say. Then the guy who sort of acted as my interrupter leaned over and said, 'Jim, we're short men here in Germany.' But I misunderstood him! I thought he said, 'We like short women here in Germany.' The woman who was talking to me was taller than I was. She still had me standing up, holding the front of my work jacket. 'You come,' she said. Next thing I knew I was getting German lessons in her feather bed!

"Her name was Ingrid. She taught English at a local grade school. She wanted to know if I was married. I figured 'what the hell,' I'm never gonna see this broad again so I admitted that I was married. 'Good!' she said. 'You stay married over in New Hampshire, I'll be your German wife!' So, for the next thirty years, whenever I went to our factories in Germany, I stayed with Ingrid."

"Uh, excuse me, James, but I believe you've told me that your wife's name is Ingrid. Isn't that right?" The other men who were drinking with the group roared with laughter. They'd heard the story before.

"Yup. But my American Ingrid is not the woman I was married to when I met the German Ingrid! Back then I was married to Margie. She died twenty years ago," Marsh said.

"Do you still see the German Ingrid when you visit the plants in Frankfort?"

"Nope. She died about twelve years ago. Now I see a German woman named Helga when I go over. Helga lived downstairs from Ingrid, so it was just kind of natural to stay with Helga after Ingrid died. Besides, Helga always babysat for our daughter when Ingrid and I wanted to go out."

"You and Ingrid had a daughter? Did Margie know?"

"Of course not! Why would she?"

"Does your new American Ingrid know you have a daughter in Germany from your other Ingrid?"

"Of course not! Why would she?"

"Does your daughter still live in Germany? How often do you get to see her?"

"Nope. My daughter lives in Boston, so I see her all the time," James said. "Look, the only mistake I made was telling German Ingrid the truth about being married to Margie. That made things a little difficult."

"Telling German Ingrid the truth about your American wife was a mistake? It made your life more difficult? How so?"

"She always bugged me to get a divorce! If I'd just told her I wasn't married she wouldn't have cared," James said.

"Did your first wife, Margie, ever suspect you had a girlfriend in Germany?"

"Nope. I had all the angles covered. Being a master electrician, I believed in closed-circuit lying. I always had my stories triangulated."

"How did you happen to marry a woman named Ingrid after Margie died? That's quite a coincidence."

"Not a coincidence at all! I sought out another Ingrid. It made things safer," Marsh said.

"Safer?"

"Yup. The German Ingrid was still alive, and I'd started talking in my sleep! It was the only time I told 'em the truth!"

James March's *First Flash Reaction* to women on two continents had ensured that he'd become a master, closed circuit liar, in two languages. He was quite proud of it.

HERNANDO GONZALEZ, 75, CASA CHICA LIES

Most of the world considers Americans to be unreasonably conservative, even puritanical, in matters concerning male-female relationships. American culture has historically embraced the *one man, one woman, married for life* philosophy espoused in the Judeo-Christian ethic that was a mainstay of life in the states right up until World War II. In the sixty-five years since that war ended, however, divorce rates have sky-rocketed, leaving many Americans to wonder if the *one man, one woman, married for life* philosophy has validity in modern times.

In the mid 1990's, I spent a great deal of time in Mexico on various consulting assignments in the automobile parts manufacturing industry. Working south of the border requires considerably more personal involvement than in the states; Mexican plant owners and management executives like nothing better than to discuss cultural differences with visitors from the United States.

During one such cultural exchange, after an elegant dinner in the home of a wealthy Mexican industrialist, the host launched in to discussion of the differences in marital practices between the two countries. It provided

WHY MEN MUST LIE

an eye-opening introspection into *Why Men Must Lie* in Mexico. There were nine men present for the discussion, seven Mexican nationals and two Americans. Our host, Hernando Gonzalez, who'd celebrated his seventy-fifth birthday just two days previously, began, "Gentleman, you know, I'm sure, that Mexico is a Catholic nation. Ninety-nine percent of our citizens say that they are good Catholics and that their priest is a very important part of their lives. But, you know, we practice practical Catholicism here in Mexico. Especially in matters of the heart!"

"Señor Gonzalez, please help our American guests understand. Remember, they are very conservative up there! Casa chica is not so accepted!" one of Gonzalez's executives said.

"But it should be!" Señor Gonzalez said. "Everyone would be so much happier! No man was meant to have only one woman! It isn't natural!"

At this point one of Señor Gonzalez's sons, Miguel, said, "Papa! Our guests may be embarrassed by what I think you are about to say! Please, Papa, let's not discuss this!"

The senior Gonzalez was not deterred. "They're men, Miguel! Of course they'll understand! They'll want to move to Mexico! Gentlemen, here in my country it is very common for a man to keep mistresses. And also very common for the mistresses to bear him children. We refer to this as the *small house* or casa chica syndrome. The more affluent a man is, the more mistresses he is likely to have! We laugh at how uptight you Americans are when one of your politicians or sports stars gets caught having an affair! Here, it would only make them more popular. Or help them get re-elected!"

"Okay, Papa, go ahead and tell them your confession story," Miguel said, to the laughter of his fellow Mexicans.

"When I was very young and just married, I went with my father to the States to a car show in Detroit. We came back through Las Vegas and spent several days there just relaxing. There were so many pretty, willing girls there that I got aroused constantly! I'd see a set of hips wiggling and boom! Hard again!"

"Excuse me, Señor Gonzalez. Would you agree that, back then, the 'Boom! Hard again' experience was your *First Flash Reaction* to all those ladies in Vegas?"

"Yes, yes, exactly! But not just 'back then'!" Señor Gonzalez said. "I still have that reaction every time I see a pretty woman; it just takes a little longer! But let me finish my story!

"When we returned to Mexico City, I went to mass with my new wife. I was feeling a little guilty about all the fun I'd had up north, so I went to confession. When I started to tell the priest about my indiscretions with girls in Las Vegas, he said, 'Hernando, Hernando! Please don't tell me about your extra women! If all the men in this church felt compelled to confess about all their mistresses I'd have to spend all day, every day in this booth, and it's too hot in here! Just confess the serious things, please!'"

Señor Gonzalez's guest all dutifully laughed at his story, but then he said, "Of course, having one official wife and many mistresses requires that a man must tell many fibs to keep things straight. But our divorce rate here is a fraction of yours in the states. Our women accept that we must lie. They don't divorce us and fatten the back pockets of lawyers."

The other American guest asked, "Señor Gonzalez, we Americans can't seem to separate lying to women about domestic matters from lying in general. Does that make any sense at all to you?"

"Absolutely none, my friend," Gonzalez said. "To place lying to women in the same category as lying in general is an American phenomenon. It's why American women are so unhappy. They've been conditioned to expect their men to do that which is unnatural. More tequila?"

ROBERT HEBERT, 77, IT WASN'T ANY DIFFERENT BACK THEN!

Many Americans like to recall the *good old days* of their younger years as a time when everything was just, well, better. They often have trouble explaining exactly what was, in fact, better or easier or more pleasant in earlier times, but still the *things were better back then* sentiment prevails. Nowhere is this more prevalent than with older men as they remember the *First Flash Reactions* of their youth.

Robert Hebert had served in Congress as a representative from

Louisiana for many terms. He was well known and well liked not only in his home state, but throughout the nation, especially in the south. During his time in Washington, Hebert had always been a friend to the military. He often visited army posts after his retirement as an honored guest of the base commander. One of these visits coincided with an army reunion I attended during which Representative Hebert *held court* after dinner one evening with stories from his long career in government.

"Hell, boys, everything was easier back when I was on the Hill! Some of my best friends were even Republicans! We'd argue like hell on the record then sit down over cocktails and hammer out solutions that worked for the nation! Nowhere near the silly, partisan bickering we see today! Particularly on matters of national security or military issues, we just did what the boys needed! Right, General?"

"Yes, sir! Sure was easier when you were on the Hill," said Major General John Moon. "You'd bring down a delegation of your fellow congressman and we'd show 'em what we needed. You never failed us. Then we'd celebrate a little, as I recall!"

Representative Hebert glanced around the room and determined there were no women with in earshot. "Yep, it sure worked better back then. No damn nosey reporters hanging around to see what they shouldn't see and stir up trouble. Ever since Clinton got careless with 'that woman,' Monica what's-her-name, thousands of so-called reporters get in the way of progress. Hell, I'd never have been elected under today's scrutiny of candidates. I liked the ladies too well! Still do!"

Hebert gave General Moon a wink when he said "still do" that was quite obvious. Another general listening to Hebert reminisce asked, "Sir, your reputation remained spotless throughout your career. Surely you're not suggesting that you were ever tempted by a pretty woman, were you?"

"A pretty woman, General? Hell no! Every pretty woman! Actually, just about every woman, pretty or not, made my head spin. Just couldn't help myself. The older I got, the worse it was," Hebert confessed.

"But you never got caught? Your wife never found out that you had an eye for the ladies?"

"Of course I got caught! Well, sort of caught. But I never admitted to anything, and nothing was ever made public. That's the difference between then and now. Back then, it was taken for granted that a man was gonna fool around every chance he got. But if he was doing his job, getting results, you know, making things happen, well, lying about matters of the heart was just overlooked," Representative Hebert said.

At this point in the conversation, two female army colonels joined in with the group of men listening to Hebert. As General Moon introduced them to the congressman one of them said, "It's a pleasure to meet you sir. We've just spent the last twenty minutes talking to your lovely wife. Congratulations on your fifty-fifth wedding anniversary! Mrs. Hebert was telling us about the world cruise you two are about to take to celebrate."

Flash: "Thank you, Colonel. She's been the only woman for me my whole life. I'd still be raising chickens in the bayou if it weren't for her. Why, the people of Louisiana still think of my Julie as their link to Washington. Yes, ma'am, she's made me the man I am today. Are you a married woman?"

"No, sir, I'm single. Hard to have time for a family when you're married to the army. Good evening, sirs."

As soon as the female officers were *clear* Hebert said, "Now where was I? Oh, yeah! I was gonna tell you guys about a little party the general and I had in Panama! Remember that one, John?"

Watching master politician Robert Hebert switch from *guy talk* to his political façade for the female colonels was amazing. After he finished his story about *good ole times* in Panama, Hebert asked General Moon, "Hey John! What's the word on that cute little colonel? She approachable?"

RAYMOND RING, 79, THE CASSEROLE KING

Raymond Ring had spent his career as a character actor. Although he'd been in many movies as a background player, he never really became a star. Raymond had, however, done literally hundreds of television commercials, so his face was well known to Americans forty years and older. Ring had been prudent with his money. He lived very comfortably in an upscale retirement compound outside Scottsdale, Arizona.

I met Ring as I was helping an uncle choose a retirement community. As we toured the pool area the salesperson introduced Ring. "And this is our resident celebrity, Mr. Raymond Ring. We refer to him around here as 'Mr. Hollywood.' All the ladies call him their sweetie!"

"Don't pay any attention to the smooth talking huckster. Which one of you is thinking of moving here?" Ring asked.

Uncle said, "I am, he's way too young. I remember you from the Ajax commercial."

"Yeah, unfortunately that's the one everybody remembers. Where are you moving from?"

"Washington, D.C. Can't take the cold weather anymore. How do you like living here? Would you recommend it?"

"Tell you what! After Miss Perfect Salesperson is finished with you, come on back out here and I'll buy you guys a drink. I'd be grateful for some guy conversation. 'Bout 90% of the residents here are women," Ring said. "Talkin' to women all the time drives me crazy!"

Ring's comment about the residents' demographics got Uncle seriously interested in the community. Two hours later, Ring bought drinks and said, "This is a great place if you don't weaken. Weather's perfect, they do everything for you, and the monthly fees are very reasonable. Are you single?"

"Widower actually. I guess that's the same thing. What do you mean 'if you don't weaken?'"

"Well, are you guys in a hurry? I mean, if you've got a little time we can grab some dinner and I'll explain the problems here," Raymond said.

"Sure, we've got nothing but time. What do you mean, *problems?*"

Over the next three hours, Ring told his story. "Guys, I'm seventy-nine years old. I don't feel seventy-nine, but when I look in the mirror I know I'm not thirty anymore. When we moved here, I was married to my wife of nearly fifty years. Alice had been in commercials, too, and we were both thrilled to leave the madness of Hollywood for the tranquility of Scottsdale. Alice died ten years ago. That's when my problems really started.

"At Alice's funeral, neighbor women begin to hit on me. All of them said they wanted to 'help me through the hard times' or 'keep me from getting lonely and depressed.' The day I buried Alice, half a dozen women brought over homemade casseroles. Everything you can imagine. Then they started showing up at my door all hours of the day and night to 'check on me!'

"I'm not going to try to sell you guys that I was a perfect husband, but I had managed to stay married fifty years! I was totally unprepared for how aggressively these women around here would pursue me."

Uncle said, "Well, Raymond, it's not the worst problem you could have, is it?"

"You ever seen a sixty-five year old woman with a bikini under her bathrobe at 11 o'clock at night, pal? Full war-paint on her face with a fifth of vodka under her arm saying she needs 'to talk?' Let me tell you, it's problems!" Ring said.

"Couldn't you just not answer your door if you don't want to be bothered?" uncle asked.

"Didn't say I didn't want to be bothered. It's keeping them straight that's a problem! I tell so many lies to so many women I can't begin to remember to whom I've told what! Half of 'em show up with Viagra and orange juice. And jealous? Man, you have no idea what's it's like when you call one by the wrong name."

Raymond seemed truly distraught by his predicament. I couldn't resist the obvious question. "Mr. Ring, if it's so bad, why don't you just move?"

"You kiddin'? This is the best place in the world. You just can't weaken and start telling them the truth. Long as you can keep 'em on their toes, you got a fightin' chance," Ring said.

"Let's go catch the salesgirl before she leaves!" Uncle said.

PETE, 81, LEE, 83, GUS, 84, AND TONY, 85
THE OVER 80 BREAKFAST CLUB

I have lived in Naples, Florida for the past five years, where I've become reacquainted with several of my older, retired male friends and associates. On the first Tuesday of every month the Naples Men's Over Eighty Breakfast Club meets at a hotel restaurant where the members can linger as long as they like after breakfast to enjoy coffee on the terrace and exchange stories. It's an informal group, not really limited to men eighty and older, and the attendance varies greatly based on the season.

During the summers when most of the *snow birds* have returned to their homes up north, the breakfast gatherings tend to be sparsely attended. That, however, doesn't limit the tale-telling time the attendees share, nor does it diminish the intensity of the conversation. I became an accepted *young guy* with the club and bore the brunt of much teasing about being *young and single* in a town where single women over sixty years of age outnumber single men over sixty by a ratio of 5:1.

Four of the regulars who seldom miss a meeting of the breakfast club are all gentlemen in their eighties. Pete, 81, was the chief executive officer of a major bank in New England. Lee, 83, retired from the air force as a full colonel and served in various duty stations all over the world. Gus, 84, is a retired precinct fire chief from Chicago. Tony, 85, owned a string of Italian restaurants in St. Louis that his sons still operate.

Pete is a widower, Lee is married to wife number three, fifteen years his junior. Gus lives with a *younger woman,* though how much younger he won't say. Tony is still married to Mary, his wife of sixty-six years.

Just prior to completing the first draft of *Why Men Must Lie,* I described the book's basic premise and content to these four men during a breakfast get together. Tony was the first to comment. "That's the problem with you young guys. You just don't know when to keep your mouth shut and let well enough alone. Why in hell would you write a book like that? Whose side are you on, anyway?"

"I gotta agree with Tony," Pete said. "What are you trying to do? Cause more trouble for all of us? I'm not in it, am I?"

Gus and Lee just sat and shook their heads. Finally, Gus said, "Okay. Let's move out to the terrace and have our coffee. I'm gonna give you a piece of advice, mister. And for your sake, I hope you'll listen. Tell me first, though, who's your target audience? Men or women?"

"Both, actually."

"Well then, you're on the wrong track right from the beginning! You know damn well that men and women have nothing in common. Especially at our age. You gotta write it for one or the other, not both!" Gus said.

"Gentlemen, do you disagree with the premise that we must lie to women, or do you maintain that men don't all lie? Remember, I've been listening to your stories for more than two years now. If I remember correctly, all four of you have told stories that support my theory."

"Well, yeah, but we never dreamed you'd write about what we said. That's dangerous!" Lee said. "You could get us all in a lot of trouble."

"Relax! Your names won't be used on your own stories. But I've got to admit, Lee's tale about when wives number one and number two met to discuss writing his biography is worthy of honorable mention for lying above and beyond the call of duty."

Gus and Pete roared with laughter at the mention of Lee's "biography" story, but Tony said, "Hey, I never heard that one. Let's hear it, Lee."

"Okay, but it's not much of a story," Lee began. "I started seeing Virginia, my second wife while I was still married to Sue. I was flying out of Andrews at the time, but flew to Wright Patterson Air Force Base regularly. Met Virginia at a bar in Dayton and started sleeping with her every time I had an excuse to overnight at Wright Pat. Then I pulled shuttle duty taking new fighters from St. Louis all the way to Nam (Vietnam) via the eastern route. That usually got me a day or two of R & R in Thailand. Did that on and off throughout the war. I divorced Sue and married Virginia right at the end of that duty. Then I got a desk job in the Pentagon for a couple of years and started fooling around with a few ladies in D.C.

"Virginia got wise to one of my girlfriends, I think her name was Cindy, and divorced me. Kind of an ugly divorce, and Virginia got so mad at me she actually called my first wife, Sue, and talked her into comparing notes on being married to me. The two of them, my first and second wives, wrote a mean-spirited biography about me and they titled it Liar Lee Lloyd, USAF. Guess it was therapy or something for the two of them. Worst part was, Sue was a pretty fair artist and she designed a book cover that featured a winged penis that looked vaguely like an F-16 with my face on the tail. They threatened to publish it in the Air Force Times, which would not have been good for my military career."

"How'd you stop them from publishing it?" Tony asked.

"I told them my current girlfriend was pregnant and that I was up for promotion to general. Then I threatened to sue 'em both for defamation of character. Doubt if they believed any of it, but they never did publish their writing."

"Good thing they didn't get to your current wife with it," Tony said.

"Naw, Sue and Virginia are both dead! My new wife doesn't even know I was married before," Lee said.

"So, Lee, you're really not in a position to disagree that men must lie to women, right?" Gus said.

"Uh, I never said I disagreed, I just don't see any good coming out of explaining it to women," Lee said. "But I'm no worse than you guys! Pete, you've brought a different lady to our Christmas party every year since I've known you. And all of 'em said you'd proposed to them."

"Hey, a man my age has a right to change his mind doesn't he? So what if I propose to them? Makes it easier to get friendly with them. I never give 'em a ring or anything!" Pete said. "But what about Gus, here? He's been living with Betty for what, eight or nine years, and she still thinks he's broke. He tells her he has to work part time so he can slip out and see Helen or Grace. One of these days Betty is gonna stop in Tommy Bahama's and catch ole Gus with one of his sweeties and a big, fat bar bill! How will you explain paying a hundred dollars for lunch when you're supposed to be broke?"

"Betty will never catch me! My buddy who really does work part time at Home Depot covers for me. Betty's called there for me a couple of times and he answers and tells her I'm in the john or running a register or something. Then he calls me on the cell and I call her right back," Gus said.

"What if Betty stopped in Home Depot looking for you? How would you lie your way out of that?" Tony asked.

"It'll never happen! Remember, we've only got her car and I always drive it. Betty's got no way to come looking for me, get it?" Gus answered. "And watch what you say about me lying, you old coot! You're the one who's had the same girlfriend for the last fifteen years! What do you tell Mary when you're seeing Mildred, Tony?"

"I can answer that," Pete said. "Tony uses me as his excuse all the time. If he'd been with me as often as he tells Mary he is, people would think we're gay, for Christ's sake!"

"See if I invite you for bocce ball anymore, Goddamn it! Now these guys will be teasing me all the time," Tony said.

At this point of the discussion a very shapely young waitress came out to refresh the coffee. "Here she is, my next wife!" Pete said. "Where have you been all my life, my dear?"

"Well, for most of your life I wasn't born! But recently, I've been observing you bring a different woman here to breakfast or lunch two or three times a week. You couldn't possibly have the time or the energy to marry me!" the quick-witted waitress said.

Over the laughter of his friends, Pete said, "But you're breaking my heart, Dear! How will I survive without you?"

"A better question would be 'how do you survive dating half a dozen different women at your age?'"

"By keeping them guessing, my dear, by keeping them guessing!" Pete said as he handed her an outrageously large tip. "Same time next week work for you, honey?"

"You and your whole group are completely full of shit, you know that, right?" the waitress said through a grin.

"That's what life's all about," Pete said. "Being full of shit, and chasing women!"

"The male and female brain are hard-wired to be different."

Dr. John Gray

Supporting Research

Fifty years of listening to men's stories made me increasingly aware that men feel they must lie to women to survive in male/female relationships. Only after reviewing and re-reviewing the hundreds of stories in my *Wives and Girlfriends* archive, however, did the depth and breadth of the lying phenomenon truly sink in. Men never spoke of being truthful and honest with their female partners. Lying to women about nearly everything, but always about their *First Flash Reactions* to other women seemed to be second nature to all men.

Prior to finalizing *Why Men Must Lie,* I embarked on extensive research in an attempt to confirm and/or dispute my findings about men's inability to be truthful with women. Was men's lying to the women in their lives really as pervasive as their own stories revealed? Had I somehow unintentionally recorded an atypical sample of stories from extraordinarily dishonest men? Did the *First Flash Reaction* phenomenon really transcend race, religion, political conviction, education level, and economic standing as the men's stories seemed to indicate? Was there any kind of scientific evidence to explain or support my findings?

The research covered a wide spectrum ranging from highly scientific explanations of why men and women behave so differently based on the physiological differences in their brains, to studies describing the effects of thousands of years of human social development on interactions between the sexes. Does this physiological difference between the sexes account for man's undeniable penchant for lying to women?

Following are a few of thousands of references to these male/female physiological brain and behavioral differences:

■ Referring to men as Martians and women as Venusians, Dr. John Gray, best-selling author of *Men Are From Mars, Women Are From Venus* writes:

"New scientific research has found subtle differences between the brains of men and women. The studies, which include both physical imaging and psychological research, are leading to greater understanding of the differences between the sexes.

While it's not completely clear how the structural differences in male and female brains affect their function, scientists theorize that the most likely impact is upon the way men and women process information.

Men's brains tend to perform tasks predominantly with the left-side, which is the logical/rational side of the brain. Women, on the other hand, use both sides of their brains because a woman's brain has a larger corpus callosum, which means women can transfer data between the right and left hemispheres faster than men. While this does not mean that women are more likely to be in their 'right mind,' it does illuminate why Martians tend to approach communication more often with a task-oriented 'let's fix the problem' state of mind, while Venusians tend to be more creative and aware of feelings in their communication style.

Martians performed better on tests requiring mental rotation, which is thought to indicate an innate sense of direction. Women, though, can rely on their stronger memory skills to help them find and remember landmarks.

However, Venusians' memory skills can be a double-edged sword, as they are more inclined to remember everything a Martian does – especially when it comes to irritating or hurtful behavior.

The other structural difference in men's and women's brains is the limbic size, which controls bonding and nesting instincts. Females, on average, have larger deep limbic systems than males. This is why Venusians tend to be more in touch with their feelings and are better able to express them than men. The larger deep limbic system also increases a Venusian's ability to connect and bond with others.

At the very least, we can gain a better appreciation for the unique strengths and qualities these subtle brain differences cause."

■ In *The Scientific American Book of the Brain*, Section IV, Behavior, Sex Differences in the Brain, Dr. Doreen Kimura states:

"Women and men differ not only in physical attributes and reproductive function, but also in the way in which they solve intellectual problems. It has been fashionable to suggest these differences are minimal, the consequence of variations in experience during development. The bulk of the evidence suggests, however, that the effects of sex hormones on brain organization occur so early in life that from the start the environment is acting on differently wired brains in girls and boys. Such differences make it almost impossible to evaluate the effects of experience independent of physiological predisposition."

- From Simon Baron-Cohen of the University of Cambridge, Bernard Crespi of Simon Fraser University, and LSE Christopher Badcock of LSE:

So what is the male brain? What is the female brain? The male brain is characterized by systemizing tendencies and mechanistic thinking. *Systemizing* is the drive to analyze, explore, and construct a system. The systemizer intuitively figures out how things work, or extracts the underlying rules that govern the behavior of a system. The purpose of this is to understand and predict the system, or to invent a new one.

In contrast, the female brain is characterized by empathizing tendencies or mentalistic thinking. *Empathizing* is the drive to identify another person's emotions and thoughts, and to respond to them with an appropriate emotion. Empathizing occurs when we feel an appropriate emotional reaction in response to the other person's emotions. The purpose of this is to understand another person, to predict his or her behavior, and to connect or resonate with him or her emotionally.

The difference between *mechanism* and *mentalism* is similar to the difference between *systemizing* and *empathizing*. In short, mechanism is about figuring things out (folk physics); mentalism is about understanding people (folk psychology).

These sex differences emerged during the course of human evolution because men and women often faced different selection pressures.

On the whole, however, these sex differences are adaptive. Men and women are different because their brains function in different ways and as a result they have different strengths and weaknesses.

- From Renato M.E. Sabbatini, PhD, *Are There Differences between the Brains of Males and Females?*

  "...aside from external anatomical and primary and secondary sexual differences, scientists know also that there are many other subtle differences in the way the brains from men and women process language, information, emotion, cognition, etc.

The conclusion is that neuroscience has made great strides in the 90s, regarding the discovery of concrete, scientifically proved anatomical and functional differences between the brains of males and females.

All the research verified that differences in male/female brain physiology and thousands of years of human interaction between the sexes have conspired and contributed to make men lie to women.

I could find nothing written anywhere declaring men to be naturally truthful and honest in communicating with the women in their lives. Nor could I find a simple, straightforward explanation as to *Why Men Must Lie.*

"Men occasionally stumble over the truth, but most of them pick themselves up and hurry off as if nothing had happened."

Winston Churchill

AND IN CONCLUSION

Please understand that I take no pleasure in divulging men's consistent lying to the women in their lives. *Why Men Must Lie* is nonetheless a phenomenon that needs to be explained. A female friend who read an early draft of the book said, "I wish someone would've told me about this thirty years ago! It makes me mad as hell, but it makes all the damn sense in the world!"

A male friend who reviewed an early draft told me, "You must have a death wish! Men will never corroborate your findings and, in fact, are going to be damn mad at you for writing this f****** book! Guys never talk about this stuff! Even though you are dead right!"

That sentiment is precisely why women need to be told the truth about their men's lying. And men, frankly, may benefit enormously from seeing themselves through the eyes of a seasoned listener and from feeling genuine empathy for those to whom they tell their lies.

When asked what single word best describes what they most want in a relationship with a man, women overwhelmingly answer, *honesty*. When asked what single word best describes what they most want in a relationship with a women, men overwhelmingly answer with two words, *great sex*. Women almost never get the truth from their own men voluntarily, but understanding the reasons *Why Men Must Lie* may enable some women to coerce honesty from the men they care about.

As evidenced in the preceding chapter, science has proven that men and women's brains are constructed differently. Centuries of societal development seem to have exacerbated these basic brain differences causing men to be more controlled by their sexual desires than women. Society has implemented structures that work to contain man's animal-like drive to copulate with as many different women as possible, but that drive continues to lurk just below the surface in every male psyche.

Following is a chronological listing of the development of male lying as revealed in the preceding stories from the seven phases of men's lives:

- At a very young age, boys instinctively understand that their natural behavior does not necessarily please their mothers.

- Telling the truth or candidly expressing wants and desires nearly always gets the boy's behavior modified by every female he comes in contact with, beginning with his mother.

- Lying develops as a necessary survival instinct as young boys interact with their mothers, trying to fit their natural behavior patterns to their mothers' expectations.

- All males are born with a gene brain function that causes them to seek quick, simple solutions.

- Lying begins with small, innocent fibs to achieve quick, simple solutions with lies to the boy's mother and teachers in an attempt to get along with them.

- Early lies are nearly always reinforced by fathers who emphasize the differences in the mind sets of women versus men.

- Fathers often tell their sons stories that *Mom wouldn't understand* or that are *just between us men*, subliminally stating that "women are too different from us to be told our truths."

- For all males, the simple life of boyhood changes dramatically when sperm production begins.

- From the time his body produces sperm, the urge to find

a sexual outlet becomes the driving force in every young man's life.

- Hiding sexual urges from Mom seems totally natural; boys don't expect that she would understand because of her past attempts to modify their behavior.

- The drive to find a sexual outlet causes every young man to experience a *First Flash Reaction* to every woman that he encounters for the rest of his life.

- In the most basic terms, this *First Flash Reaction* is every male's involuntary, natural first brain impulse in the presence of a female, i.e., what do I have to say or do to get along with this woman well enough and long enough to have sex with her?

- Beginning in the later stages of Phase I and becoming entrenched during Phase II, males begin to understand that the sexual drive that motivates their every thought and action is not shared by the women they find so irresistible.

- Early fibs to his mother and teachers conditioned the boy to lie to bridge his perceived gap between what women expected of him versus what he wanted to do.

- The young man *naturally* lies to achieve his all-consuming drive for sexual intercourse.

- Once a man experiences that first fantastic orgasm with a woman, his *First Flash Reaction* to other women intensifies into the single, most all-consuming, *must repeat as often as possible* objective that he will pursue for the rest of his life.

- Men have fundamentally different feelings about virtually every aspect of life than women do, but seldom are willing to confront those opposing feelings head on (Silent Lying).

- As men mature, they find it progressively more difficult to tell women what they are truly thinking and feeling; what they really want (more Silent Lying).

- Lying becomes a natural reaction for men to get what they want the simplest way.

- Men tell three basic types of lies to get their way and/or to avoid doing things they don't want to do:
  - Overt Lies
  - Borderline Lies
  - Silent Lies

- Some men become much better at lying than others; all men intuitively understand they must become reasonably proficient liars to survive their interactions with women.

- Men find themselves lying to women easily and conveniently about nearly everything, but always about everything concerning sex.

- Men feel the need to lie to women even more as they get older.

- Men are as uncomfortable communicating openly and truthfully with women at age seventy-five as they were in Phase I, when they were less than twelve years old

- During Phases V, VI, and VII lying to women becomes a game with many men, even as they find themselves ever more dependent on the women in their lives.

STATED MORE CONCISELY:

- Men are conditioned from birth to lie to women to get what they want.

- As boys mature the one thing they want more than anything else is sexual satisfaction.

- For males, every other want and need takes a distant second place to the drive for sexual gratification.

- The vast majority of males have an overwhelming in-born desire to experience sex with as many women as possible, searching to repeat that *first fantastic orgasm* experience again and again with additional females.

- Only fear of consequences prevents men from pursuing multiple female sex partners.

Like it or not, men are conditioned from birth by women to lie to women, beginning with their mothers. This conditioning is an unintended consequence of women expecting boys and men to see the world as women see it. This simply never happens.

To reiterate, I report these findings with a great deal of trepidation. A lifetime of listening to men candidly reveal their inner feelings, however, has convinced me that the basis of misunderstanding in male to female communication is rooted in men's total lack of motivation to be truthful.

Men, quite simply, are conditioned to lie to women to get what they want, and to avoid what they don't want. What men want most from the time they experience that *first fantastic orgasm* is to repeat that *first time* experience with as many women as possible. Lying to his wife or current female partner about his need to repeat that *first time fantastic orgasm* with other women is the root of adult male dishonesty.

Remember that men have the potential to lie to women about everything, but the vast majority of lies men tell involve their *First Flash Reactions* to other women whether acted on or not. Men simply are not comfortable being honest about their sexual wants and needs with their girlfriends and wives from puberty forward. This sets the stage for lying consistently about virtually everything. Men rationalize total lying by reasoning that if they have to lie about their desire for other women, they might as well lie about everything else as well.

Does the male lying documented in *Why Men Must Lie* mean that a man does not love and respect the woman he's with? Does his deceit infer that he doesn't care enough about his family and home to jeopardize them by being untruthful? Does a woman's need for total honesty make it virtually impossible for men to be truthful?

Most men claim that they do, in fact, love and respect their wives or female partners even if they cannot give them the total honesty women so desperately desire. Even Bold and Aggressive and Consistent, Careful Liars don't want to lose their homes and families despite their inabilities to control their *First Flash Reactions* to women. Nearly all men claim they wish they could be more honest with the women in their lives.

Is there, then, any light at the end of this tunnel of deceit outlined in *Why Men Must Lie?*

Yes, but it is a perilous journey with an extremely challenging qualifier that few women are willing to address.

A woman must empower her man to be able to speak truthfully about everything, beginning with his *First Flash Reactions* to other women, and still get what he wants.

If a man knows unequivocally that he can confess his attraction to other women, his need to repeat that *first time fantastic orgasm* with other women, without his wife or girlfriend coming completely *unglued*, he may gain the capability to be truthful about nearly everything. He must be convinced that his partner understands and accepts that his most basic, sexual *First Flash Reaction* to other women is as basic to his existence as breathing; a condition he cannot change.

If, however his wife or girlfriend insists that he deny his *First Flash Reactions* to other women, she is laying the groundwork for deceit that will transcend through all of his communications with her, forever. The woman must create a situation where her man can openly transfer his *First Flash Reactions* to other women back to her alone. If a man can become comfortable being absolutely honest about his sexual needs and desires, there is some probability that he can learn to be truthful about everything else.

Every woman absolutely must understand that, no matter how fervently their husbands or boyfriends swear otherwise, men are first and foremost driven by sexual desire. All other emotions are secondary to men, period. Only if his wife or girlfriend enables him to be absolutely candid about his true *First Flash Reactions* to other women can a man begin to be truthful and forthcoming about other aspects of life.

■

Women: Your man's brain is physiologically different than yours. Your sons' brains are physiologically different than yours. Male brains function in a simple, linear fashion. From puberty until death male brains are primarily driven by sexual desire. Accept it; you cannot change this condition, but you may be able to help the men you care about minimize the pain it causes you and other women.

Your sons start becoming sexually driven males at a much earlier age than you want to acknowledge. Accept this in your sons and stop trying to make them see the world your way. Their future wives will be forever grateful to you if you can condition your sons to express their sexual desires honestly, clearing the path to truthfulness with women about everything else.

Recognize and accept the sexual animal that is in your man. Forgive him for lusting after other women because no woman can erase that from any male persona. Create an environment that will bring him back when he strays. Forgive him his indiscretions, if you can. He has been conditioned from birth that you want to change him; stop trying.

If a man must lie to you about his *First Flash Reactions* to other women, he feels justified, *vindicated* to lie to you about everything else.

■

Create an environment that gives him the courage to tell you the truth about his *First Flash Reaction* to every woman he encounters and you may get what you want most, total honesty!

"Lies are essential to humanity. They are perhaps as important as the pursuit of pleasure and moreover are dictated by that pursuit."

Marcel Proust

www.ingramcontent.com/pod-product-compliance
Lightning Source LLC
LaVergne TN
LVHW051508080426
835509LV00017B/1976